The Thankful Principle follows Marcia Day Brown's life-changing journey into thankfulness. While frustrated and dealing with a troubled teenage daughter, the author reluctantly began thanking God in the midst of trying circumstances, according to Philippians 4:6-7. Feeling empowered, she began applying it to other areas of her life. Dramatic results followed. Through sharing her testimony with friends, strangers, on the mission field of South Africa, and even in a women's prison, the Thankful Principle is continuing to change lives today.

Marcia Day Brown is a wife, mother of four, community college instructor, and freelance writer/editor. Her freelance career has included writing top-selling greeting card and poster editorial, a newspaper column, advertising, and editing work. She is a graduate of Evangel University with a B.S. degree in Elementary Education.

THE THANKFUL PRINCIPLE

A Journey into Thankful Living

by Marcia Day Brown

Thankful Press

Copyright © 2013 Marcia Day Brown

Cover Design by Tracy Johnson, CIRCA (circadigitalgroup.com)

Cover photo by Todd Johnson, CIRCA (circadigitalgroup.com)

For more information, contact:
Thankful Press
Indianapolis, IN
davmarbrown@sbcglobal.net

Publisher's Cataloging In Publication Data
Brown, Marcia Day, 1964 –
        The Thankful Principle: a journey into thankful living / Marcia
Day Brown.
        perfect bound.
        1. Biographies & Memoirs – memoirs. 2. Religion & Spirituality –
Christianity. 3. Self-Help – personal transformation; relationships; stress
management. I. Brown, Marcia. II. Title.

TABLE OF CONTENTS

Author's Acknowledgments

Danielle, my precious daughter, thank you for graciously allowing me to share our struggles. Without your permission, this story would never have been told. I love you and am excited and proud that you are now embarking on your own journey into thankful living.

To my other three children, Jessica, Jacob, and Laura, thank you for bringing love and joy into my life.

Thank you to my husband, David. You are the love of my life, and I am blessed with God's best for me. Thank you for asking total strangers (my parents) in 1987 to pray with you for a "Proverbs 31 wife" to share your life with.

Thank you to my parents, Dr. Gene and Jill Day. You have always been godly examples in my life and an encouragement to me.

Thank you, Mom and Jan, for reading through my manuscript.

Emily, thank you for being obedient to God in joining me, Jacob, and Laura on the mission trip to South Africa.

Thank you to Todd and Tracy Johnson, my friends from CIRCA (circadigitalgroup.com). Tracy designed my amazing cover, and Todd snapped the gorgeous front cover photo.

I would especially like to thank my friends and family members who have shared testimonies with me and kindly allowed me to share their stories. You have spurred me on to continue sharing my testimony with others.

CHAPTER ONE
VICTIM OF CIRCUMSTANCES

IN THE SPRING OF 2004, a typical weekday morning took an unpleasant, dramatic turn. I was heading to my teaching job at a local community college and planning on dropping my fifteen-year-old daughter, Danielle, off at our local high school. Although I don't recall exactly what I said or did in the minivan that morning that ticked her off, some sort of argument ensued. Typical. It seemed as though every time I turned around, there was some sort of major upset or drama with this child. My daughter was constantly lashing out at someone: her younger brother Jacob, little sister Laura, her father, or me.

At times, I wondered if this was typical teenage behavior or whether we were dealing with some other unexplained issue. It felt like I was living with two different people. My daughter could be sweet and enjoyable one minute and angry and moody the next. Whatever the root cause, it was beginning to take a toll on our entire household. My younger children would often be upset with their sister or reduced to tears, and my husband and I had begun experiencing greater tension between us, too. It seemed my angst-ridden daughter was keeping our entire household in a constant state of turmoil.

During these tense, difficult months, I would frequently question my skills as a parent and ask myself and God, "Why is this happening? What have I done to deserve this?" It seemed so unfair. I had begun feeling like a victim of circumstances. Poor, miserable me would often host a pity party. Mentally, I would remind myself that I had been a good daughter to my parents (and, consequently, didn't deserve this situation based on my past wrongs), and I was a pretty good mother to my children, too. Nevertheless, I was constantly crying out to God and asking, "Why? Why? Why?" Some days I just wanted to crawl into a hole.

After I had dropped Danielle off at school that unfortunate morning, I seethed inwardly, "How dare you start my day like that!" I was extremely angry, especially considering the fact that my day was already going to be stressful, since I was going to be giving final exams to my college math students that day.

Immediately, the thought crossed my mind, "*We wrestle not against flesh and blood.*" Ephesians 6:12 had popped into my head, and it immediately made me feel defensive.

"It sure feels like I'm wrestling my flesh and blood," my mind argued.

Within a split second, a portion of another scripture crossed my mind. This passage had gotten me through tough times before, and it came back to me again that day at a time I really needed it: "*Do not be anxious about anything, but in every situation, by prayer and petition, with thanksgiving, present your requests to God. And the peace of God, which transcends all understanding, will guard your hearts and your minds in Christ Jesus"* (Philippians 4:6-7, NIV).

My mind then flashed back to the many times I had called my parents to complain about some situation, and they would usually reply, "Praise the Lord. Are you thanking God yet, Marcia?" I found their frequent urgings and cheerfulness a bit annoying at times. I didn't need a guilt trip, when I just wanted a sympathetic ear. Couldn't they just let me vent? It's hard to praise the Lord when the car breaks down, the kids get sick, or there is an unexpected expense, but at that moment, something clicked in my mind. If I was supposed to come before God with "thanksgiving" and make my requests known to him, then that must mean I would have to THANK him for the problems. After all, if there is a request, it generally means that there is a problem involved that needs solving.

Since I was alone in my car and still in an angry frame of mind, I began shouting in my car: "Thank you, Lord, that Danielle has a crummy attitude! Thank you, Lord, that you're going to send people across her path today! Thank you, Lord, that you're going to be our testimony!" I probably shouted out several more bits of thanks to God in those few moments and said whatever came to mind.

If anyone in a passing car had noticed me yelling and gesturing, they may have thought that I looked like a crazy woman, but I didn't care. I felt like the kid who has finally had enough of the school bully and begins to take action by swinging his fists and hoping he hits something. Please note that although I was angry about the situation, I was not mad at God; however, I was mad at the devil. Consequently, each time I yelled my thanks to God, I felt like I was punching the enemy and giving him a busted lip or a bloody nose.

It was quite therapeutic. The next thing I knew, I began feeling a little cocky. Inwardly, I pictured myself looking like a boxer, dancing around and taunting his opponent by saying, "You want a piece of me? You want a piece of me? Just try to get me, punk! I'm not scared of you!"

A new resolve replaced the victim mentality that I had been operating under for months. That day I served Satan notice that if he tried to get at me again through my children, I was going to start thanking God EVERY TIME, whether I felt like it or not. It was like I had suddenly gotten this clever idea and was boasting to my enemy by saying, "Yeah, I'm going to start thanking God. What do you think about that, Devil? I'm not going to take this from you anymore!" No longer was I going to be bullied or a victim of circumstances. I didn't have to take this lying down, but I could now do something proactive and give the enemy a black eye in the process. It was freeing to recognize this truth, and this realization transformed my thinking about dealing with difficult circumstances.

Surprisingly, after my "scream fest," I began to experience a strange sort of peace, the peace that "transcends all understanding." It didn't make sense, but I was no longer feeling angry. In fact, I had a fantastic day and was pleased to learn that Danielle had also had a good day that day at school. I thought to myself, "It works!"

Although it didn't all happen overnight, this experience was a revelation of God's truth that would continue to grow and change my thinking. In the days ahead, I would cling to this truth to an even greater extent, and it would transform my life. This was the beginning of the Thankful Principle.

Chapter Two
Practicing Thankfulness

A FEW DAYS after my morning commute revelation, Danielle and I were tangling again at home over some minor issue. As usual, she began mouthing off in typical teenage fashion. Mentally, I began replaying my scream fest episode from the car, "Thank you, Lord, for Danielle's crummy attitude. Thank you, Lord, that you're going to send people across her path. Thank you, Lord, that you're going to be our testimony." Within seconds, my daughter suddenly grew quiet.

"Wow," I thought to myself, "this really works!"

On another day, as she was yelling at me on her way up the stairs, I began repeating the same thankful words under my breath. Again, she immediately stopped. It was like I had discovered a new secret weapon in dealing with my difficult daughter. It amazed me how quickly a volatile situation could be diffused by simply thanking God.

A few days later, I had a misunderstanding with my husband, Dave, on a Sunday morning. Because I didn't want to go to church in an angry mood, I wondered if the Thankful Principle would work on my marriage. I began to thank God for the misunderstanding, for my overreaction, and for making me human. Within a few moments, I began to feel at peace again. God then gave me wisdom and insight into handling the situation, which involved humbly going to my husband and apologizing for my part in the flare-up. Again, it worked and harmony was restored.

I began making a mental note of these small successes in thankfulness. Although I wasn't practicing the Thankful Principle consistently, I began to see that God could use my thankfulness for a problem to change me, the situation, or both. No matter what the outcome, peace always followed.

One day, I told Danielle about what I had been doing in regards to thanking God for her negative attitude. It wasn't long before I found myself separating her from her younger brother. Rarely did my kids get into physical confrontations, but this time I was peeling her off of my son's back and breaking up a fight between the two of them. I was fuming mad and prayed out loud, commanding Satan to take his hands off of my daughter in the name of Jesus and for the peace of God to reign in my household.

Smirking, Danielle smugly asked, "So, are you thanking God yet, Mom?" She was so good at finding ways to push my buttons, and this really irritated me.

"No," I replied curtly, "but I will. Thanks for reminding me!"

I did begin to thank God for the problem and also thanked God that he was the solution to the problem. Then a miracle happened. We had thirteen days in a row of peace in our home. It was amazing, especially when I considered the fact that we were pretty much having daily explosions and outbursts from our moody teenager. I viewed those thirteen days of peace as a major victory and praised God.

Although, we still had emotional outbursts from time to time, I had begun walking in the knowledge that I did not have to be a victim of circumstances. When I remembered to thank God in the midst of the trying circumstances, God could bring peace to me and my family's situation. It transformed my thinking about dealing with difficult situations within my home.

During the summer of 2005, a year later, I was planning a family trip to Hawaii with Danielle, Jacob, and Laura to attend a 50th anniversary celebration for my parents. We would also spend time at a reunion with all of my four siblings and their families. Altogether, there were 36 of us (including the 24 family members who were residing in Hawaii). I was nervous about whether Danielle and I would be able to avoid major drama while living in close quarters for about eleven days, but I did have my secret weapon with me. I had prayed before the trip even began, and every time some minor flare-up would begin to occur during the trip, I would quietly pray and thank God for the situation and thank him for restoring harmony. In doing so, I experienced peace in the matter and avoided getting sucked into an argument or fight. When I would begin to thank God at the least little sign of disharmony, it seemed to head the problem off at the pass. Our entire trip was a blessed time of family unity, and I was so relieved that God worked everything out so beautifully.

CHAPTER THREE
NEW APPLICATIONS FOR THE
THANKFUL PRINCIPLE

OVER THE NEXT COUPLE OF YEARS, I began finding new ways to apply the Thankful Principle. With my husband's commission-based sales job, some months were leaner than others. At one point in time, our finances were strained, and as we were going through this stressful episode, I had begun thanking God for the situation and experiencing a peace about our finances. This was unlike me not to stress and worry, since I was the one writing the monthly checks for our bills.

I was concerned about my husband's worries over money one morning, and I told him, "Dave, I feel a peace about this situation, but I want God to help you to experience it, too." I prayed with him and asked God to give him the same peace that I was feeling. I just knew that God had everything under control, but Dave was stressed. About an hour later, I went to work at a library sales exhibit for a part-time job that I had with a book distributing company. When I got there, my boss excitedly let me know that they had just received payment from a school library sale that I had made a couple of months earlier for a large order, and they were going to write me a check that day. It was more than enough to take care of our pressing needs at that moment, and I was rejoicing that God was right on time. I couldn't wait to call my husband to share the good news and was thanking the Lord the entire drive home.

Another time, I applied the Thankful Principle at work. In my job as an adjunct mathematics instructor at a community college, I had begun growing steadily frustrated with my department chair at that time. She had been dividing up classes in a manner that did not seem fair or considerate to veteran instructors. At times, I received fewer hours than someone newer would get, or I would get a class time that interfered with my family life and told to "take it or leave it." Other times, it seemed we just didn't see eye to eye on policies in place. I was fed up and practically ready to quit, and this was affecting my attitude. However, God showed me that I needed to thank him for the situation, and he even encouraged me to treat my boss with more respect, which I began to do.

Within weeks, my boss was transferred to a position she liked better in another department, and I ended up with a chairperson who was a dream to work with. I began getting fuller teaching schedules that worked well with my family's needs, and I even felt more appreciated and respected by my new boss. And because I had treated my old boss with more respect before her change in positions, I was able to maintain a degree of cordiality with her whenever our paths did cross.

Another semester, it looked as though my schedule might not come together at all. I was worried that I might not get a full schedule or even workable hours. I began grumbling in the faculty workroom. Within minutes, I felt conviction over my actions, and I repented and asked God to forgive me for my grumbling. I prayed, "Lord, I thank you for this situation. You know what classes I need. You know which students I'm supposed to have. You know what finances we need, and I'm going to trust that even if I get fewer hours, you are going to take care of our finances through Dave's increased sales or in other ways."

About five or ten minutes later, I received an e-mail from my dream boss, and she had given me a list of classes to choose from that worked out well for my schedule. Not only did I get to pick my own classes, but I also got a full load of classes, plus one extra class. God's goodness and faithfulness amazed me.

I was so excited about the results I was seeing when I began walking in thankfulness. It wasn't long before I began sharing my thankful testimony with others and inspiring them to use the Thankful Principle.

CHAPTER FOUR
THE VALLEY OF THE SHADOW OF
DEATH

IN THE FALL OF 2007, my husband had me rush him
to the doctor's office to check out a mysterious
pain in his upper right quadrant. With his medical
background as a former x-ray technologist, he was
certain it was an acute case of appendicitis. After
tests were run, appendicitis was ruled out;
however, after a follow-up with his general
physician, it was suggested that David should go
ahead and have a colonoscopy. Just shy of his 49th
birthday, he was nearly at an age that one is
routinely recommended, so it made sense to go
ahead and schedule the procedure.

I had to work the Friday morning of the
colonoscopy, and I actually didn't expect anything
major to come from it. Since Dave didn't want me to
have to take off from work to go with him, he had
arranged for a friend to pick him up after the
procedure. Because he was still semi-drugged from
the procedure, he was glad that his colleague Harry
was able to hear the consultation report with him;
otherwise, he might have been a bit foggy on the

details of the procedure. Although Dave didn't recall saying it, Harry later remarked that after the diagnosis, Dave had expressed relief that he had taken out an additional term life policy the previous year.

As soon as I finished teaching my morning class and was heading home, I called my husband and cheerfully asked him about the results of the procedure. Dave's answer struck me as sort of strange and vague, since he suggested that he would tell me more about it after I got home. Immediately, my antenna went up, and I realized that something was wrong. My mind was racing a mile a minute, as I immediately thought the worst. Fortunately, I was five minutes from home when I spoke with him, and I anxiously rushed into the house after I pulled into the garage.

When Dave sat down and talked with me, I learned that the colonoscopy had revealed a cancerous tumor in his colon. We were to meet with a surgeon in a few days and schedule the needed surgery as soon as possible. Thanksgiving was only six days away, and we were wrapping our heads around a cancer diagnosis. At the time, we weren't feeling very thankful, only numb.

When we shared the news with our three teenage children at home, as well as our married daughter, Jessica, in Florida, I could sense their worries and fears about their dad. Tears filled the eyes of the girls at home, Danielle and Laura, as they gravely considered the possibility of losing their father and how it would impact them. Jessica was a bit choked up on the phone and worried about her dad, too. Our son Jacob seemed to take the news better than his sisters did, but he was also concerned.

Since my husband works as a financial planner,

he sat down alone with me that weekend and discussed matters that we would often think about only in an abstract sense, matters that are supposed to be for some time off in the distant future. His words took on new meaning in the context of our current situation, and I sensed the gravity of the matter. It was surreal when my husband explained the particulars about the insurance policies he carried on his life and the investments we had together. Wisely, he even mentioned which colleagues he trusted in the event of my becoming widowed. It was practical on his part, but I didn't really want to consider the potential outcome of losing David and planning for a future without him.

I don't know exactly when I started applying the Thankful Principle, but early on, I began to thank God for the cancer diagnosis and thanked God that he was going to get us through this terrible situation and would be our testimony. This was something I could be proactive about and not allow myself or David to become victims of circumstance. As I continued to thank God, I felt strongly that this would be a temporary hurdle, and I was confident that my husband would survive.

One night, however, I did begin to allow worry to creep in about the fact that Dave would have a lot of down time from work. With his job being in sales, I knew that this down time would mean that he wasn't out making sales. How would we deal with this financial setback? It wasn't as though he got sick pay in his line of work. This was one reason he rarely took vacation time.

God knew exactly what I was thinking and reminded me of a familiar passage from Matthew. *"Therefore I tell you, do not worry about your life, what you will eat or drink; or about your body, what you will wear. Is not life more than food and the body more than clothes? Look at the birds of the air; they do not sow or reap or store away in barns, and yet your heavenly Father feeds them. Are you not much more valuable than they? Can any one of you by worrying add a single hour to your life? And why do you worry about clothes? See how the flowers of the field grow. They do not labor or spin. Yet I tell you that not even Solomon in all his splendor was dressed like one of these. If that is how God clothes the grass of the field, which is here today and tomorrow is thrown into the fire, will he not much more clothe you—you of little faith? So do not worry, saying, 'What shall we eat?' or 'What shall we drink?' or 'What shall we wear?' For the pagans run after all these things, and your heavenly Father knows that you need them. But seek first his kingdom and his righteousness, and all these things will be given to you as well. Therefore do not worry about tomorrow, for tomorrow will worry about itself. Each day has enough trouble of its own"* (Matthew 6:25-34 NIV).

I didn't know how God was going to do it, but after rereading the passage, I felt encouraged that God would take care of our family's needs. I made a decision that I would not waste any more of my time and energy worrying about the matter any further. God had promised to take care of us, and by faith I received that word.

The day before Thanksgiving, we met with the surgeon and discussed Dave's surgery. Anxious to operate as soon as possible, the doctor set a surgery date for the following Monday, November 26th. Since that was the day before our 20th wedding anniversary, I made a lighthearted remark to Dave, "Way to get out of taking me out to dinner for our anniversary, Honey!"

Without missing a beat, he chimed back, "Yeah, but you can have all the hospital Jell-O you can handle."

Over the next few days, we could literally feel the prayers of the people who were praying for us. I had always heard people describe such a feeling, but I could never truly relate to their stories until I had experienced it myself. As I continued to pray and thank God that he was going to help us through Dave's cancer situation, a strange thing happened. The day before my husband's surgery, not only was I not worried, but I felt a joyful anticipation and a sense of excitement that God was going to bring good from our situation. I couldn't wait to see what God was going to do through this experience, as unpleasant as it was at the time. Whatever happened, I knew we were going to have a testimony to share when it was all over, and I was excited about that.

In a way, I felt a little guilty that I was feeling a joyous sense of expectancy, rather than feeling stressed and worried. It didn't make sense to others, and it certainly didn't even make sense to me at the time. However, that joyful feeling continued to encourage me in the challenging days and months ahead. When I would feel discouraged, I would remember that indescribable surge of joy and hope that I had experienced at the time of Dave's surgery.

On the day of Dave's surgery, it was moved up to earlier in the day than originally planned. I was scheduled to teach a class at that time, but since my in-laws were with him at the hospital, Dave decided to proceed without me. I arrived before it was over and was thankful that I didn't have to spend the entire surgery in the waiting room. He made it through the ordeal and then spent the next six days in the hospital. I spent the first night in his hospital room, which was the closest thing we had that year to an anniversary getaway. In fact, I had even joked about it by making a big deal out of it and commenting about my "swanky accommodations" in the newly remodeled hospital.

After midnight, I noted to the nurse that it was officially our 20th wedding anniversary. While Dave was still sedated and sleeping, I told the nurse about the Jell-O crack Dave had made a few days earlier. Afterwards, she looked at me seriously and inquired, "Would you like some Jell-O?" I thanked her, but declined.

That night was a rough one for me because I had gotten a flu shot at my annual physical on the morning of Dave's surgery date, and I must have been having an allergic reaction. I told the nurse about my flu shot and tetanus booster shot because I was worried that I might end up passing out or have difficulty breathing. Thankfully, after a long nap at home the next day, while my in-laws hung out with Dave at the hospital, I was back in good health. This was not a time I could afford to be sick.

A few weeks after Dave's surgery, we met with the oncologist for the first time to discuss his treatment options. We learned that Dave had been diagnosed with Stage III colon cancer. Since that stage was the next-to-the-worst stage for a cancer diagnosis, the news was sobering. The oncologist recommended an aggressive form of chemotherapy, which would be administered every two weeks for about five months. On this schedule, Dave would spend every other weekend getting his chemo treatments. He would then feel ill for a few days and begin to have a few good days just before his next round of chemotherapy.

Poor Dave had to endure this terrible cycle of taking drugs that made him terribly sick, and just when he was feeling better again, he would have to start the whole routine over again. It was somewhat depressing for him having to face each new round, like having to face the stomach flu every two weeks. In addition, the treatment also had an unpleasant side effect of causing neuropathy (a tingly numbness) in his upper and lower extremities, such as in his fingers and toes. He was told that it would most likely go away after a year or two, but in a small percentage of cases, it could be permanent. Throughout it all, he was a trooper and rarely complained or seemed to feel sorry for himself.

About a month after Dave's surgery, Danielle, age 19, made the decision to move out of town to work, go to school, and live in her own apartment in an area about 200 miles away. She wanted to return to where we had lived during her childhood. Although the Thankful Principle had helped our relationship in numerous ways, she was still a willful teenager and butting heads with us regularly. As her mom, I worried about her making it on her own, but I was also thankful that her decision to move out and spread her wings did bring some needed calmness to our home at that time, which helped in Dave's recovery.

During the months of Dave's chemotherapy treatments, he was working approximately half of the usual amount of time that he would have normally spent working outside of our home. He also managed to keep himself busy working on home remodeling projects on the days he needed to stay home. Miraculously, during the spring of 2008, Dave wrote higher sales figures than he had during the previous spring sales period. Even though he had spent considerably less time out in the field, somehow the amount of his commissions had improved dramatically over the previous year. God reminded me that he had kept the promises that he had shown me months earlier from the book of Matthew. I had been told not to worry, and I marveled at God's grace and provision. In the natural, it made no sense that my ailing husband generated higher sales numbers that spring, but with God all things are possible.

Dave spent much of the year convalescing from the colon cancer surgery, and at the end of 2008, he had a second surgery. This time it was to repair a hiatal hernia. Although it should have been a routine surgery, scar tissue from the previous surgery made it difficult for the surgeon to stop the internal bleeding. Blissfully unaware at the time, I didn't realize how close I came to losing my husband until sometime after the surgery.

Over the next few months, Dave encountered many difficulties in his recovery. His surgery had an unexpected result that was something similar to what a gastric bypass patient might experience. He had to learn to eat differently and subsequently ended up losing about eighty pounds over the next year or so and went down three shirt sizes to a medium. In addition, the continuing neuropathy in his fingers and toes were cause for frustration.

I worried about him, especially knowing that his health was somewhat fragile from both surgeries and the chemotherapy. During those months of recovery, I continually prayed and thanked God that we were going to get through our present situation. God calmed my fears and gave me peace every time I would turn it over to him. I just had to remember to do it.

CHAPTER FIVE
MY TESTIMONY AND FACEBOOK

IN THE SPRING OF 2009, I was inspired by someone else's experience of reconnecting with old friends on Facebook and opened up my own account. Although I had previously told my kids that they didn't "need" Facebook and tried to discourage them from using social media, I soon realized how much fun it was to find old college and hometown friends. I spent a great deal of time catching up online and enjoyed the virtual reunion experiences, and my kids loved ribbing me about my new hobby by throwing my words back in my face. I guess I deserved it.

One of my hometown schoolmates was a great resource for filling me in on the lives of our mutual classmates and friends. We spent a couple of days writing detailed private messages back and forth to each other, and we had such fun reading our newsy notes. At the time, her older daughter had recently moved back home, and my daughter Danielle was moving home, too. Danielle had been away a little over a year, but because her job situation didn't work out and a relationship had ended, she was reluctantly ready to move back home at the age of twenty.

My hometown friend and I had each shared concerns about our headstrong daughters, and I ended up feeling inspired to share my thankful testimony with her. Although I didn't even know her religious views at the time, I felt strongly that perhaps my friend needed to know my story and that it might encourage her when dealing with her own frustrations and worries concerning her daughter. Nervously, I awaited her response.

When I did hear back from her, I was greatly relieved when she started out the message favorably. She responded, "Marcia, okay, I am not sure I would have accepted the advice to thank God from many people, but it hit home coming from you somehow." She shared that as a Catholic, she had not spent a great deal of time studying scriptures, although she would hear them in her church services. She said that personally studying and familiarizing herself with the scriptures was something that she was trying to rectify in her own life. Later she added, "I went upstairs and got my bible and looked up the passage that you quoted. I like the idea and will try to put it into practice —it definitely sounds better than being mad all the time. I don't normally talk religion to most people. I find it to be something personal. I did not find it offensive for you to tell me that, however. It is a quality in you that I have always known and accepted."

She went on to thank me for sharing my story with her and told me, "I will let you know how it goes." I was excited that my pal had taken the story to heart and was going to try the Thankful Principle, too. I could hardly wait to hear her good report.

I responded to her decision to try it by replying, "I got tears in my eyes when I read your note. I hesitated about sending the last note, but just felt in my heart that perhaps you needed to hear my story. People can argue religion and theology, but one cannot argue personal experience. Thank you for taking it to heart. I'll be anxious to hear your results!"

The next morning, I added to my note in the Facebook messages I was sending to her. I commented, "When I got up this morning, I went back and read all of Philippians, chapter 4. A couple of things stood out to me. The first thing that I noticed was that in verse 4, Paul says to 'Rejoice in the Lord always. Again I will say Rejoice.' That's just a couple of verses before he says to come before God with 'thanksgiving.' I guess if we're rejoicing 'always,' then we can't help but come before God with thanksgiving when we make our requests known. Further in the passage, Paul mentions something about learning to be content, no matter what his situation. (Paraphrase on my part.) Anyhow, it all went with the earlier verses in that Paul had made rejoicing and thanking God a way of life; therefore, it changed him to be able to have contentment in his life. I've read that passage many times, but this was the first time I saw the big picture in how taking his own advice affected the Apostle Paul's life and would have a transforming effect on others."

My friend replied, "I read the entire passage as well last night. I said many thank yous as I was falling asleep."

I had shared my thankful testimony with my friend because of her daughter's recent move back home, but something else interesting happened. My friend had been dealing with a painful, pinched nerve for over a month at the time I shared my testimony with her. When she studied the passage in Philippians and began thanking God, something moved in her neck, and she was suddenly healed from the pinched nerve pain. I'm not even sure if she was thanking God for the neck pain or for the situation with her daughter, but in the midst of thanking God, she was no longer living with the pain and was miraculously healed.

That same week, I listened to a song on a Christian CD that moved me. I shared my thoughts with my friend, "I went to pick up Jacob this morning, and I had a Christian CD playing that belonged to Laura. It has a song that came out a few years ago, called 'You Were There' by a group called Avalon. Something in the song resonated with me this morning, and I had joyful tears streaming down my cheeks and felt like I was having a worship service right there in my car."

At the time, I felt like God was emotionally preparing me for Danielle's move home. I had concerns on how things were going to work out, and the ministering quality of the music seemed to prepare me for the rocky road ahead. I had begun thanking God in advance to avoid the potential storms I knew were approaching. I thanked God that he was going to work things out in my relationship with my daughter and thanked him that my daughter was coming home.

On the day we moved Danielle home, it did not go as smoothly as I would have planned. I sent my friend the following private note: "Pray for me. I've had a trying afternoon. Let's just say that Danielle had some upsetting news when I got down here that was related to a poor decision. I am already thanking God in the midst of circumstances and feel better. We will get through it, and it's not nearly as bad as what another friend of mine is going through. I just got word from a friend in New Zealand that her 19-year-old adopted Romanian daughter (who has an identical twin) was hit by a car Thursday night and is not expected to survive."

How could I feel sorry for my own situation when another friend's child was hovering between the balance of life and death? My friend eventually lost her lovely daughter, Natasha, and was devastated, but I still had mine in one piece. I was not happy with choices my child was making, but I was thankful (when I remembered to thank God for the situation) and asked God to help me guide my troubled daughter, who was still in the process of finding herself and spreading her wings. Over the next few days and weeks of conversations and comments with my hometown friend, we became a mutual encouragement to each other, reminding one another to be thankful. One day she told me, "I have thanked God for you today." Another day she wrote, "I hope you had a good start with Danielle coming home. It is a good thing you have your thank yous to help —you will need them."

I responded, "Believe me. I am thanking God a great deal since Danielle has been home. Jacob is also going through a weird phase emotionally, but is still a good kid. I am praying for him often, though, since he is moodier and is lacking in direction to some extent. In addition, he is questioning his values, morals, world view, etc. It's normal, but I want him to come out of this phase unharmed." I went on to speak of other family news, and at the end of the note, I added, "Thanks for your friendship. I'm thanking God for you regularly now."

Yes, I was thanking God a great deal after Danielle moved back home. She was an adult, but I couldn't help but be concerned if she was out late, and I didn't happen to know where she was. She spent most of her days working or spending time out late with friends, so I rarely saw her when she first moved home. Even though we had some guidelines, there were many times that I was worried about her or frustrated, and all I could do was thank God and put my daughter in his hands.

At a later date, my hometown friend shared, "Glad to see a post from you this morning. I was thinking about you as I was reading my lent book and saying my thank yous! Can't say I feel calmer, but I am still working at it. I'm not exactly stressed either, so maybe it is helping." Months later, she added, "I passed on your 'thankful' prayer to my cousin today."

For a while, it seemed that I was sharing my testimony with many other friends on Facebook, whenever I felt someone needed an encouraging word. Remarkably, God can turn our trials into our testimony, and it is beautiful to see the results. I began referring to these times of sharing as my "Facebook ministry." Whether someone was going through a divorce, having trouble with kids, or dealing with discouragement, I knew that the Thankful Principle would give them hope, too. A number of friends were receptive to my story and thanked me for sharing it with them. Every time God nudged me, I shared my testimony of thankfulness with anyone who would listen.

CHAPTER SIX
MORE DRAMA

In May of 2009, I was planning a road trip with my younger two children, Jacob (17) and Laura (15), to visit my parents in Kansas. One evening, Laura came downstairs with tears streaming down her face, sobbing uncontrollably, as if her heart was breaking. I was puzzled at what could be upsetting her so dramatically. She then went on to tell me that she had just heard the shocking news that an upperclassman high school friend, Maggie, had been tragically killed in a car accident that afternoon. Jacob was also shocked at the news, since Maggie was a friend of his, too, and in the same grade. In fact, he knew that he had possibly been the last one chatting with her online, just before she left to give a friend a ride home from an after school tutoring session. How could someone, who was just communicating with him only a few hours earlier, be gone so quickly? It was a sobering thought.

Both of my children were attending a small charter school with less than 200 students at the time, so the loss was emotional for them and the entire school. Everyone knew each other.

Understandably, both of my kids wanted to attend the funeral, which was going to occur during our planned trip. I had also heard rumors that some of the kids wanted to gather at the corner of the accident scene to have a vigil of some sort the next night, but it wasn't really a safe place to gather.

It was obvious the classmates needed a place to grieve, and my children wanted to do something positive with their friends and be part of some sort of tribute for Maggie. As a family, we discussed the situation and talked about the fact I didn't want to cancel our trip or have them gather at a dangerous intersection, so I offered a compromise. We would invite the kids from school over to our house that Friday night for a cookout, and they could use our home for a safe gathering place and remember Maggie.

Danielle, Jacob, and Laura all pitched in to clean the house for the event, and I knew that we had made the right decision to have the open house. However, in the midst of our preparations, tempers started to flare, and I realized that I needed to seriously start thanking God again. The thought crossed my mind, "Do you see what is happening? The enemy is attacking, and if order is not restored, **you can't bless people tonight."** Under my breath, I began to thank God for my children and their crummy attitudes and thanked him for restoring peace to my home. I genuinely wanted the presence of the Lord to be in our home that evening, so I discussed this desire with my children. We needed to put the anger and harsh attitudes aside and allow God to use our gathering as an opportunity to minister to those who were lost and hurting. I sternly reminded them that God could not use us, if we allowed the enemy to spoil our attitudes, preparations and plans. After a somewhat tense discussion, they reluctantly agreed, and we had no more drama between ourselves that day.

We had no idea how many people would be coming because the invitation was spread by word of mouth and social media, so I had to guess on the number of guests to prepare for. About thirty to forty of my kids' classmates ended up coming that evening, and the opportunity to just hang out together as a group was comforting in their time of grief. As God always does when he lays something on my heart, he made sure that I had more than enough of everything to take care of our guests.

Although Danielle did not know Maggie, she had graciously made a simple DVD video that featured pictures of Maggie. She had set it to a musical background and played it for everyone in our living room. That evening several individuals shared their memories of Maggie with me and spoke about their own feelings at the loss of this fine, young Christian girl. By the end of the evening, I felt like I knew her, too. I heard stories that indicated that much in Maggie's life seemed to be in order, including the fact that she had thoroughly cleaned her room the night before the accident and had also recently been baptized.

Everyone thanked us for hosting the event, and I felt a sense of gratitude that God had allowed us to be a part of the healing process in these young people. For some, it opened the door for friendship with my children and even with me. Several allowed me to pray with them and were receptive to my words of hope and encouragement. Others later (to my children's chagrin) sent me friend requests on Facebook. I never sent them requests, but if they asked me, I accepted and occasionally shared advice or wisdom with them from time to time.

In the weeks and months that followed, I witnessed how this one tragic event positively impacted the lives of my children. A few weeks later, Danielle went on to make a more elaborate pictorial DVD for Maggie's family in time for what would have been her June birthday. This led to Danielle finding a creative passion and later pursuing a major in graphic design. Jacob had been both comforted and troubled about his last conversation with Maggie and even questioned whether prolonging that conversation might have saved her life. We both knew that he couldn't go back and change things, but I did notice that he seemed to snap out of the negative teenage phase he was going through and began to grow stronger in his faith and character. Laura seemed to have a heart to reach out to the friends of Maggie who were still hurting, including the survivor who was with Maggie at the time of the accident. Although they were all older friends, she gave them wise counsel and even asked for me to buy a bible for a school friend who needed one or offered to give someone a ride to church.

During the summer months, Danielle's presence back at home was at times causing stress and friction, as she had been away for over a year and used to answering to no one. By early August I had just finished my summer session of teaching, when Danielle made a startling announcement to me and Dave. We were upstairs in our bedroom, and I was doing something on the computer, when I turned around in my chair to listen to what she had to say. She nervously informed us that she was newly pregnant and had just confirmed her condition a day or so earlier with multiple pregnancy tests that all came back positive.

At first, I thought she was joking, since she had made such remarks in the past to get a reaction out of me. This time, she indicated that she wasn't kidding. I was beyond surprised and immediately angry at first. I didn't even know she was dating anyone, but apparently, she had been seeing Eric for a few months and had known him for years. He was a musician and skateboarder, and he seemed a little rough around the edges to me—a guy who marched to the beat of a different drummer. He was living in our neighborhood and had also recently moved back home months earlier around the time Danielle did. Danielle wasn't necessarily hiding the fact that she had been seeing him, but it just never came up in conversation.

Outwardly, Dave took the news more calmly, but inwardly, a storm was brewing inside of him. On the other hand, I vented immediately and launched into a very tense conversation with my husband and daughter. Under the circumstances, it was a fairly normal reaction for a mom caught off guard.

Understandably, her father and I were both upset with the news and had questions, but it wasn't long before I finally calmed down and started to pray and thank God later that same day. "Thank you, Lord, that this baby is going to be a blessing to our family. Thank you, Lord, that we will be a blessing in the life of this child. Thank you, Lord, that you're going to be our testimony. Thank you, Lord, that you are going to be glorified in this situation and bring good out of it."

Although I was still somewhat in shock, I did begin to feel an inner peace when I made a point of thanking God in the midst of this trying circumstance. What else could I do? It was a relief not to have to go through this on my own, but with thankfulness on my part, God always brought peace to my heart and eased my worries. A few days later, Danielle, Jacob, and Laura flew out to visit their sister Jessica's family in Florida, where Danielle broke the news of her pregnancy to all three of her siblings. With the kids out of town, this meant that Dave and I had a few days alone to sort out our feelings and to talk about Danielle's current situation. We were both still experiencing raw, mixed emotions at the news.

A variety of feelings run through a parent's mind when an unwed child announces an unplanned pregnancy: anger, shock, embarrassment, concern, excitement, frustration, hurt, disappointment, and even joy. I experienced all of these feelings and more. A few days after the kids left for Florida, Dave and I took a weekend road trip to Kentucky and Tennessee. Tough times can either bring a couple closer together or tear them further apart. We were determined to do the former. Our extended time in the car allowed us an uninterrupted opportunity to freely talk in depth about our thoughts and feelings about the new grandchild, our concerns for Danielle, and how the changes were going to affect us and the rest of the family. More than a few tears were shed that weekend.

When we got over our initial outrage and frustration, we were able to work on our relationship and become united in our support for Danielle and the new baby. It would not be easy having an infant under our roof again, but we would be there for our daughter and grandchild. Once I got used to the idea, I was even looking forward to the arrival of a new grandbaby. Actually,

I think I was more at peace with things before Dave was, but we prayed together that weekend and put the situation in God's hands.

As I was continuing to pray for Danielle over the next few weeks, I felt that God had given me a word that the baby was going to be a girl and that she was going to be feisty. When I told Danielle the news, she was excited at the prospect of a daughter, but she wasn't sure about the last part—that worried her a little. A few months later, an ultrasound did reveal the sex of the baby as a girl.

In the fall of 2009, Danielle returned to school, so that she could stay on our health insurance plan. Although she was reluctant to return to college, she knew she needed the insurance. This time she began pursuing a visual communications degree with a concentration in graphic design. I was thankful Danielle was back in school and began thanking God for the young man in her life, who had never been to church at all until after Danielle's pregnancy was announced.

Danielle and her boyfriend, Eric, had a very challenging relationship. It ran hot and cold for many months. Danielle did not want to get married just because she was pregnant, and although she wanted her baby to have a father, she hadn't completely made up her mind that Eric was the man with whom she wanted to spend the rest of her life. Eric, who did not know his father and had not been raised with a father figure in his life, was determined to be there for his child and supported Danielle's decision to keep the baby. The two of them had many things to work out in their relationship, which was filled with many ups and downs.

Over the next few months, Eric began to grow on

me in positive ways, as he slowly became a part of our family. For Danielle's sake, he started attending church and even made some sort of commitment to Christ at one service. I began talking to him more regularly and finding out more about him, and I glimpsed that behind his musician/skateboarder exterior was an intelligent, personable young man. He definitely was a unique individual and had his own ideas about things that differed from mine, but he seemed to love my daughter and was excited and nervous about becoming a father. I grew to like and care about him.

Early in Danielle's pregnancy, I learned that Eric's mom and I shared the same birthdate (although mine was three years earlier). I noted that it was a strange coincidence that both grandmas shared an April 6th birthday, and since Danielle's due date was April 17th, I kept telling her for months that she would have the baby on our birthday. Sure enough, late on the evening of April 5, 2010, I drove Danielle and Eric to the hospital. Feeling victorious about my prediction coming true, I chanted gleefully, "The baby's going to be born on my birthday! The baby's going to be born on my birthday!"

Laura and I both wanted to be there for the baby's arrival, so we kept vigil at the hospital all night, but the baby took her time arriving. We both had school and work the next morning, but we returned to the hospital during breaks in our day. As it turned out, I ended up missing out on Chloe's early evening arrival because I was teaching a night class, but I loved the fact that I shared my birthday with my precious granddaughter, Chloe Layne. She was a great 46th birthday present. Now I would have an excuse to be a kid again on my future birthday celebrations.

As I was driving to work the next morning, I was marveling at the fact that my tiny granddaughter shared my birthday. I wondered if my positive confessions had caused this to happen or whether God just wanted to grant me a little desire of my heart. One of my favorite scriptures says, *"Take delight in the Lord, and he will give you the desires of your heart"* (Psalm 37:4, NIV).

I thanked God for this latest blessing. Of course, I had been thanking God for Chloe for nearly nine months, but it was thrilling to finally meet her.

CHAPTER SEVEN
HOPE FOR THE HOPELESS

VIRGINIA, AN ELDERLY FRIEND FROM CHURCH, invited me to join her in participating in a once-a-month women's prison ministry. One Sunday night per month, this particular group would be in charge of a service at the Indiana Women's Prison, which was located near downtown Indianapolis at the time. I had been reluctant to join, but after meeting some others who were part of the group, I decided to accompany her to a service.

The first few times I went, I could do it without certain credentials, but I would eventually have to get a special badge and go through a more thorough screening process, if I were to continue working with this ministry on a regular basis. During my first visit, I was a bit nervous. What would it be like spending time with such a large gathering of female offenders? In the service itself, I saw only one or two guards keeping an eye on things, but there were probably over one hundred inmates at the service. I wondered what would happen if things got out of control. Was it really safe to even be there?

All of the inmates wore tan uniforms. If I hadn't

known that I was in a prison, no one would have stood out to me as a hardened criminal. They didn't look much different than folks on the outside, except for their matching uniforms.

I don't recall if it was at the first or second service I attended, but at one of them, I had been asked to play the piano and sing a song I had written. One of the inmates helped me get set up at the keyboard with the microphone. She was so sweet, articulate and helpful, and I could picture myself being good friends with such a person in my daily life. I couldn't imagine what she must have done to wind up in prison, and I didn't ask her; however, I would later be surprised to learn that she was in prison for murder.

After I had shared my song during the service, I returned to my seat. An inmate tapped me on the shoulder and said quietly, "You just made my friend cry." I was touched by her remark and glad that the song was a blessing to someone in the service.

Years earlier, I had recognized the fact that music can minister to and touch someone's heart in ways that words alone cannot. I could tell someone in a song, "Don't throw your life away. You can clean the mess you've made," and they could receive it because their defenses would be down. I could say personal things in a song that I could never have said to a person's face without making them feel defensive and drawing an angry response. Many times I had shared songs that had been written in my times of feeling hurt, experiencing loneliness or seeking the will of God, and it wasn't unusual for someone to tell me that a song brought healing or encouragement.

From my first visit to the women's prison, I knew

in my spirit that one day I would share the Thankful Principle with these women. Several times I shared my music with the women, but I had never been asked to speak. After my first three visits, I had to go through the process of filling out paperwork, attending a training session, and obtaining the proper documents to officially become a volunteer with the prison ministry. It took the better part of a Saturday to get everything in order, but I knew that I was supposed to do it.

Although I wasn't able to attend every monthly meeting on a Sunday night, I did attend when I could. One Sunday, I was running a bit late and wasn't sure if I would even get to Virginia's house in time. I prayed about it and asked, "Lord, do I need to go tonight?"

"You don't have to go," was his reply.

Relieved, I decided not to go and was starting to think about evening plans, when God continued, "You don't have to go, but I'd like you to go."

Obediently, I told the Lord that I would hurry up and get ready to go.

When I arrived with Virginia at the prison and was checking in with the other women, a funny thing happened. The guest speaker wasn't allowed in that evening because her name was not on the gate release. This caused the woman in charge that night, who was filling in for another leader, to wonder aloud what we were going to do that night for our main speaker.

I knew this was my opportunity. Before anyone else could make a suggestion, I immediately spoke up and volunteered, "I have a testimony that I would like to share tonight, if you'd be willing for me to speak."

"Do you have a scriptural passage to go along

with it?" she asked.

"Yes," I replied, "Philippians 4:6-7."

Relieved at my offer, she decided that I would deliver the message that night. I knew that it was no accident that God had told me that he wanted me to come that night. I quickly went and read through the scripture passage that I wanted to share and prayed that the message would go well and reach receptive hearts.

Nervously, I stood in front of the congregation of inmates and began telling the story of my journey into thankfulness. After I got started, the jitters went away, and I was able to thoroughly enjoy sharing my story and the scripture passage with the women gathered that evening for the service. I started with the story of the morning scream fest in my minivan and then shared other experiences in my life where the Thankful Principle had worked for me and for others.

At times, I got downright animated, and I would ask the crowd, "And do you know what I did next?"

The group would enthusiastically respond, "Started thanking God."

"That's right," I would reply, "I started thanking God."

I shared about Dave's cancer. I shared about my unwed daughter announcing her pregnancy. I shared about my struggles, and I shared with them that God did not do this just for me because I'm someone special or more deserving than anyone else. I let them know that God wanted to do the same for them, too, if they would come before him with thanksgiving and make their requests known to God. If anybody could relate to being a victim of circumstances, these women most certainly could, so I challenged each of them to trust God and to begin thanking him for the problems in their lives every time they felt like a victim of circumstances. I told them that I was expecting to hear good reports from those who would try it.

After the service that night, a couple of the women shared with me that they felt that the message I had shared was just for them. One was having challenges with a teenage daughter at home, and she could relate to my story of trials with Danielle—only she was dealing with her daughter's problems from inside the walls of a prison and felt helpless to guide her daughter back home. I encouraged her and gave her a hug that night before I left. Virginia told me afterwards that it was obvious that my story was connecting with the women in the service that night, and I praised God that he had laid it on my heart to come and had given me the opportunity to share that night, even though it meant the other speaker had been inconvenienced.

I never did return to the monthly women's prison meetings. Shortly after I spoke, the women in that prison were transferred to another facility further from my home, and God did not lead me to continue participation with the prison fellowship group. I had accomplished the purpose there that he had planned for me at that time.

In remembering this period of ministry, I am mindful of the words of Jesus concerning the matter of ministering to those in prison: "*Then the King will say to those on his right, 'Come, you who are blessed by my Father; take your inheritance, the kingdom prepared for you since the creation of the world. For I was hungry and you gave me something to eat, I was thirsty and you gave me something to drink, I was a stranger and you invited me in, I needed clothes and you clothed me, I was sick and you looked after me, I was in prison and you came to visit me'"* (Matthew 25:34-36, NIV).

As Christians, we often think that ministering to prisoners is someone else's job, but we are all called to this work. We can easily agree to feed the hungry, share drink with the thirsty, bless a stranger, provide clothing, and help in times of sickness, but ministering to prisoners makes us uncomfortable. That's how I used to feel, too. I understand.

If a willing heart will start out with something small, like sending a letter to someone who is in prison or supporting a prison ministry, this can be a path toward future prison ministry. God can always use a willing, obedient heart. When the timing is right, I am sure that I will have the opportunity to minister to those in prison again and will gladly do so.

CHAPTER EIGHT
BABY DAYS

AFTER CHLOE CAME HOME from the hospital, we had not only added her to our household, but Eric took up residency, too. Obviously, he would not be sharing a room with our daughter, so he slept on our downstairs couch. I had originally been under the impression that this was going to be temporary and only for the first few days that Chloe was home; however, it suddenly became necessary for Eric to stay on a more permanent basis. I asked Jacob if it would be okay for Eric to share his room, and he agreed to do so.

Having four young adults, ranging in age from 16-22, an infant, and two middle-aged adults living under one roof was a real challenge. Many days and nights, I was thanking God for helping me to keep my sanity. I loved bonding with Chloe and rocking with her for hours, and the entire family pitched in and helped out with Chloe when Eric or Danielle had to work or go to school.

We settled into a semi-normal routine, but it was stressful. I found myself constantly juggling work and household responsibilities in addition to babysitting duties. We were in survival mode, and

Dave and I had little time alone. We found ourselves going on dates just for a cup of coffee in order to have uninterrupted conversation alone.

Another addition that year to our household included a rescued dachshund, whom we named Brutus. I never intended to add a dog to our household, after having to put a previous dog down years earlier. However, a couple of months before Chloe's birth, Jacob decided to sneak two pet rats into his room. He had been given the rats and a large cage and managed to slip everything into the house one day while I was at work. When I got home from work that evening, he led me outside the door to his room. Before he opened the door, he remarked, "You're probably going to kill me, but..." This led to the "big reveal."

Well, I was furious when I saw the rats, so I didn't even want to speak to him at that moment. I just marched myself out to the car and drove around the block a couple of times to cool off. I knew I needed to extricate myself from the situation before I said some things I might regret later. I don't recall whether I began thanking God at that moment or not, but when I did return home somewhat calmer, I made it very clear to my son that he was not going to keep those animals and would have to locate a new home for them.

This event led to my husband mentioning a rescued dog he had seen at a vet's office where he had made a business call. After some discussion, I sensed that my husband really wanted a dog and reluctantly agreed to allow the little guy a home on a trial basis. Although Brutus was an additional new responsibility and an expense, he was a calming influence on Dave, who was still recovering his health. Since Brutus was pretty much an older lap dog, who generally led a life of leisure and enjoyed snuggling, Dave found that gently stroking the dog was relaxing in the midst of our chaotic household. He credited the dog with lowering his blood pressure, too.

After fifteen years of going without a dog, even I had begrudgingly grown to love and care for our new pet, too. If someone had told me I would be capable of caring for an animal to the point of being crazy about him, I might not have believed it, but it wasn't long before the dog was accompanying me on errands, sleeping in our room, and even tagging along on our vacation with us. Dave used to joke that he liked Brutus because he was the only member of the family who didn't talk back. Some might even suggest that Brutus rescued us, rather than the other way around. He did add some joy to our home during this period and became a treasured member of the family.

Over the next few months, Danielle and Eric were busy parenting Chloe and attempting to find time for each other around their scattered work and school schedules. As with most young couples, friction and conflict was normal; however, it was not always easy to avoid commenting or sharing advice when one side or the other would share grievances or concerns with me. At other times, I might be caught right in the middle of an argument and feel more like a referee in a battle zone. When I remembered to start thanking God, the situation would generally calm down quickly.

One evening, Danielle was extremely upset after a verbal spat with Eric, so she angrily left the house and slammed the front door behind her. Right after that, Eric bolted out after her. Since the pair had left abruptly, I was left holding the baby. I began to pray, "Thank you, Lord, for their crummy attitudes. Bring peace to this situation. I thank you that you're going to be our testimony in this situation, Lord." And then a miracle happened. Within minutes, not only did Danielle and Eric make peace with each other and return to the house, but Eric came to me and humbly apologized for his part in the scene I had just witnessed. I was amazed and knew that God had definitely intervened at that moment.

When I would hold or rock my grandbaby Chloe, I would often sing to her and talk to her, reminding her that I was thankful for the blessing she was to our family. I loved being able to grandparent Chloe on a daily basis and formed a special bond with her. She was living proof that God can bring something positive out of a difficult situation, but I worried at times over the fact that my granddaughter might not grow up in an intact family. I continued to thank God that he was working on this situation and that he was going to be our testimony.

Eric did begin making some personal improvements for the sake of his family. He got a G.E.D. and began taking some college classes, and Danielle completed her associate's degree in visual communications. In spite of these gains, the stresses of work, school, and parenting took a toll on the young couple, and they broke up before the end of 2011. By that time Chloe was twenty months old and too young to understand what was going on with her parents. It was not an amicable break-up, so Eric hurriedly moved out of our home and into his own apartment.

Danielle was hurting and finding herself, besides clashing with her father and me more, too. By

February, we all agreed it was time for Danielle to get her own place, but we wondered how she would be able to afford it on her income from working as a stylist in a children's salon. A few nights during her transition after the breakup, she even slept at a close friend's house to have some space away from us, while we took care of Chloe. It was easier than clashing with each other, and I thought it was important to maintain some stability for Chloe's sake.

In my hunt to find affordable living space in a decent neighborhood for my daughter, I discovered information about some area apartments that offered a discount on the rent, based on income. When Danielle and Dave went to look at the complex, she loved it; however, she was disheartened to learn that the waiting list was eighteen months or so for a two-bedroom unit. Disappointed, she went ahead and added her name to the waiting list and hoped something would open up sooner. During this time, I frequently thanked God that he was going to work things out for Danielle to have an affordable and safe place to live, and I believed and thanked God that he was going to be our testimony. I knew the time was right for her and Chloe to have their own place.

The next day, a phone message for Danielle was left on our answering machine, but it was the following morning before I noticed the blinking light. Apparently, the apartment complex had a three-bedroom apartment that no one on the waiting list could take at that time. Would she be interested in it? The rent was slightly higher, but it was still affordable enough for her to manage. Within two days of being told that she would have to wait eighteen months for an apartment, Danielle was offered an even nicer, more spacious unit than the one she had requested. We praised God and saw his hand in the entire situation. I was amazed at the speedy answer to prayer, and we were all pleased with the quality of the apartment unit.

The apartment was in a lovely neighborhood and conveniently located near our church and wonderful shopping districts. Located about fifteen miles away from our house, the new apartment was just far enough away from home to give her a bit of space and independence, but close enough to obtain free babysitting help from family members when needed. God seemed to be blessing Danielle abundantly during this time, but in contrast, Eric was struggling.

I was not happy with some of the choices Eric was making after he moved out of our home, but I continued to pray for him. Even if her parents were not together, I wanted Chloe to be safe and happy when spending time with either parent, so it was important to thank God for the situation and trust him. Just around Chloe's second birthday, less than four months after their break-up, Danielle and Eric began to work on their relationship again. Skeptical, I was cautiously optimistic that Eric had changed, and I hoped that he was truly on the right track. Was he really changing, or was he just trying to win Danielle back? Only God knew the answer, so all I could do was continue to pray.

CHAPTER NINE
LOSS AND GAIN

RIGHT AROUND THE SAME TIME that Eric and Danielle were reconciling in the spring of 2012, Dave's seventy-five-year-old father, Norman, was hospitalized. It sounded serious, so Dave, Laura, Danielle, Chloe, and I drove to the hospital in Illinois to pay him a visit. We were worried about his health, and while I prayed for his healing, I was more concerned about him spiritually. Although he had attended church in his younger years, he had not been one inclined to go to church in his adult years or even talk about spiritual things around us. I thanked the Lord for the chance to visit with him, and I prayed that if God would provide an opportunity and the words to say, I would talk to him about my concerns about the state of his soul.

When Dave and the girls took my mother-in-law, Wilma, out to lunch, I volunteered to stay behind and keep Norman company. Inwardly, I was thanking God for the opportunity to speak with my father-in-law, but I was also a bit nervous and praying for the right words to say to him. When we were alone, I somehow managed to steer the conversation toward spiritual things, and I commented to him, "Norm, your grandkids are worried that they aren't going to see you in heaven someday."

He quickly dismissed my comment and began talking about the many Christians he had known, especially those in leadership who were hypocrites in his opinion. I listened to his words and heard about the hurts and disappointments he had experienced earlier in life. I reminded him that we couldn't totally base our relationship with God on other people and explained to him that if he truly wanted God to reveal himself to him, all that he had to do was ask. I told him that he could do it sometime when he was alone, and I shared that if he sincerely wanted to know God, he should ask God to reveal himself to him. Inwardly, I kept praying that the words would sink in and thanked God for the opportunity to speak candidly with my father-in-law.

Later, the rest of the gang returned, and before heading home, Dave asked his dad if we could pray with him before we left. He talked to his father about salvation, but told him that we weren't pressuring him to make a decision that day and that we just wanted to pray with him and bless him. His father agreed to let us pray with him, but he wasn't willing to make any sort of commitment that day. Dave's prayer was touching and eloquent. Tears streamed down his father's face, and he told Dave afterwards that it was the most beautiful prayer he had ever heard prayed. The rest of us were also misty-eyed by the time Dave finished praying.

His father went home from the hospital shortly after our visit, but within two weeks, he was rushed back to the hospital again. This time, things seemed more serious, so Dave and I took Jacob with us on that Mother's Day Sunday. We weren't sure how much time he had left, so we wanted Jacob to have an opportunity to see him, since the girls had joined us on the previous visit.

While there, we learned that things were looking grim for my father-in-law, and I continued to pray and thank God in the midst of this trying circumstance. I repeatedly prayed for God to reveal himself to Dave's dad. Our visit was emotional, as we could tell that Norman was trying to get out his good-byes to us in person. It was sad to see his health deteriorating and to witness his frustration over the option that morning of a Popsicle for breakfast when he wanted to be given real food. He had so much he seemed to want to say to us that day, and he even took a few moments to have meaningful conversations over the phone with our oldest daughter, Jessica, in Florida and a niece, Kathy, in Mexico. He made a point of reminiscing and telling both women that he loved them, and he seemed to tear up and become misty-eyed during his conversations. His niece told him that when he got to heaven to be sure and hug her mother, June. Norman had been especially close to his older sister, June, and he had keenly missed her after her tragic death in an auto accident fifty years earlier. Before he hung up, I overheard him telling his niece, "Your mom would have been proud of you."

Again, we prayed with him before we left that day, and tears flowed down Norman's cheeks. On our way home that Sunday evening, I called Jessica and let her know that things were not going well and that we weren't sure how much longer Grandpa would still be with us. She immediately made plans to fly up with her family to see him on Friday. By Wednesday, we were receiving word that Norman would be transitioning to hospice care, but within a couple of hours, he had suddenly passed away.

We were shocked to lose him so quickly, since we had initially thought it might be a matter of days, weeks or even months. For our children, his death was their first experience with the loss of a grandparent, so it was especially hard to take. My heart ached for Jessica and granddaughter, Kylie, who weren't able to see Grandpa Brown and hug him one last time. Dave and I stayed up late talking and reminiscing with each other and the kids at home.

Although we were saddened by the loss of Dave's father, who had always been a hardworking, loving dad, we were thankful that he was no longer in pain. It had been difficult to see him face certain indignities and struggles near the end of his life. Strangely, though, I felt an almost surreal sense of peace during this time. My heart felt an assurance that Norman had made his peace with God and that God had indeed revealed himself to my father-in-law. I thanked God for his love and faithfulness.

A couple of days later, I was lying in bed and thinking about the amazing peace I felt about Dave's dad and his passing. I asked God about it, praying, "Lord, I feel such a sense of peace in this situation. Is it just me, or is Norm really with you in heaven?"

Immediately, I felt the same calm assurance and sensed his reply, "Yes, he's here with me...and he's hugged June, too!"

I could hardly wait to tell Dave's cousin, Kathy. Thankfulness filled my heart, and I rejoiced that I had a reassurance that my dear father-in-law was truly at peace and with God for eternity. I shared my thoughts with my husband, as we made preparations to return to Illinois for the funeral, and it seemed to bring him some comfort, too.

Jacob had also experienced a sense of peace in his grandfather's passing. He had been fervently praying for him near the end and had felt an assurance that his grandfather was in heaven, too.

While at the funeral home visitation, we had an interesting conversation with Dave's older cousin, Charles. Charles was also concerned about the state of affairs in Norman's spiritual journey, and he felt strongly that he needed to visit Norm in the hospital that Wednesday. Just hours before Norman's death, Charles had gone to the hospital to visit. While there, he spoke frankly with some concern and said, "Uncle Norman, I'm just going to come right out and ask you something. Are you saved?"

Norman replied calmly, "Yes, Charles, I'm saved."

His story brought immense comfort to my children and granddaughter Kylie. Kylie, age 7, had been especially worried about her great-grandpa and whether she would ever get to see him again in heaven. I thanked the Lord for the additional confirmation and the joy that followed.

In addition to our four children, two granddaughters and son-in-law, Derek, Eric also accompanied us to Illinois for the funeral. He wanted to be there emotionally for Danielle and to help with toddler Chloe. At the funeral dinner, a cousin was taking group pictures of my mother-in-law, her three sons, me, our children, and grandchildren. Eric started to stand off to the side, but my mother-in-law told him, "Eric, get in the picture. You're Chloe's father, so you're family." I appreciated the kind gesture, and I knew she meant it. I think it also touched Eric to be included as part of the family, and he did join us for family photos.

Eric returned to church that summer and had even been counseled some by our pastoral team. Although he was only a decade older, our pastor told Eric that he wanted to be a dad to him. He wanted to guide Eric and encourage him in his Christian walk. The mission statement of our church talks about "fathering sons and daughters into the kingdom of God," and it is a commitment that our pastor and others in the church have taken seriously through fellowship, teaching and discipleship. Eric also joined a small group for men, and they were involved in a Christian book study and learning to be godly men and leaders. As a result of participating in the group, Eric began to change in positive ways. The connection and fellowship within a brotherhood of spiritual men truly did something constructive that encouraged this fatherless young man and inspired him to desire to become a leader to his family and to make better decisions for himself.

That summer, he began taking courses at the college for a certification program in heating, ventilation and air conditioning. Dave helped him to acquire some of the needed tools, and I made sure he had a ride home from classes. Eric seemed to take the classes seriously and passed the coursework, so we were all pleased with his maturity and progress.

One evening near the end of summer, he was skateboarding in a store parking lot, after he had gotten off from work at a nearby restaurant. An older man walked up to him and told him that he felt like the Lord had a message for him. Without even knowing whether or not Eric was a Christian, he went on to tell him that God was "proud of him" and to "keep on the right path." He went on to say to Eric, "You're going to reach people that I can never reach."

While they were talking, another man walked by and said something. Eric immediately recognized him as our former pastor, who had been leading the church a couple of years earlier when Eric had made a commitment to Christ during an alter call. Eric said, "Hey, you used to be my pastor." The former pastor didn't recognize Eric, until he was reminded of how Eric had come to the church with our family three years earlier. He said a few encouraging words and left. The first man asked Eric if he could pray with him, and after they prayed together, the man left.

About ten minutes later, another older man walked up to Eric and delivered a similar message to what the first man had said. He told Eric that God was proud of him and to keep on the right path, and he also told Eric that he would be reaching people that he could never reach. This man also prayed with Eric before departing. Eric was both puzzled and blessed by the strange occurrences, which he later related to Danielle.

When Eric and Danielle ended up sharing the unusual story with Dave and me at a restaurant a few days later, we were both pleased and surprised. I reminded Eric that the fact that he had been encouraged by three separate men was definitely not something to be taken lightly and that God was probably trying to get his attention. In my mind and heart, the stories were also a confirmation to me that Eric was changing for the good. Not only did he take his role as a Christian man more seriously, he had started sharing his faith with his non-Christian friends and was inviting them to church. A few even started attending the small group book study for men that he had attended a few weeks earlier. He was definitely reaching people that others could not reach, and it was exciting to see the positive changes in him. We were proud of him, and all we could do was thank God.

CHAPTER TEN
MY STUDENT AND THE THANKFUL
PRINCIPLE

ON THE FINAL EVENING of the semester, I was grading the last of the exams for my night class and sharing the results with one of my female students. I had honestly enjoyed having her in class because she was one of my more dedicated students in that particular group and personable, too. Although others had fewer responsibilities, this gal in her thirties juggled being a wife, college student, and a mother to five children and still managed to make good grades.

My student passed my class with a decent overall grade, but she was disappointed in the score she made on the final exam. We were alone at the time, as the other students had already turned in their tests and left for the evening. Philosophically, she commented that her score wasn't too bad, when she considered the stress she had been under at home during the last few weeks of the semester. Since we were alone, she began to share some of the issues she had going on in her marriage, and she told me more about her background and her life outside of school. Faith and family were important to her, but she was at risk of losing her marriage, unless something changed with her husband.

I asked if she had a few minutes, which she did, and then I began to share my thankfulness testimony with her. She was moved and encouraged by my account. In addition, I prayed with her before we departed and agreed in prayer with her that her husband would be open to attending a men's group at church that would help him deal with certain issues in his life that were hurting his family. She had planned that evening to discuss the idea of him joining the men's accountability group and was glad to have me supporting her in prayer on the matter.

Although I felt good about our time of sharing, I did not expect to hear anything further from her. The semester was over, and I figured we would go our separate ways; however, I got an unexpected e-mail from my student two days later with the following message:

Marcia,

> *I cannot thank you enough for praying with me on Wednesday. It was just what I needed. I've tried the thankful prayers and haven't seen any huge changes, like you had, but I'm going to continue with that. I do find that if nothing else, it does change my attitude. I did express to my husband how important it was to me for him to attend the men's group coming up this month, and with some hesitation, he has agreed. It's really huge, though. He's somewhat overwhelmed with the commitment because the men commit to meeting for a year to work through their issues. At least he knows*

*upfront that this isn't going to be easy. I bet the
enemy will probably work overtime on him on
therapy days, so I will especially be praying for
him then.*

Talk to you soon,

R---

*P.S. It's refreshing to have a college
professor/instructor that is a Christian. Sometimes
it's hard to sit under someone who is an unbeliever
and their worldview spills out into class
instruction.*

I was so thrilled to hear the results of praying for
my student's husband and thankful that God
answered our prayer. The following week, I got
another exciting e-mail from her reporting more
good news. It was wonderful to see that my student
was actually applying the Thankful Principle and
learning firsthand the blessings of thanking God in
the midst of a trying circumstance.

Marcia,

*I have to share. Maybe you can add this example to
your testimony, and I will definitely add it to mine.
Last night my hubby was trying to print something.
His computer would not connect to the wireless
printer, and it kept giving him error messages. He
couldn't save the file either.*

*He began his tirade of cursing and grumbling,
slamming his mouse and other things on his desk.
He continued to gripe about how messy and
unorganized things were and that he could never*

get anything done, and he didn't understand what was wrong with his computer. I offered a helpful comment, telling him I remembered him having trouble with it the other day.

He continued, while I was soaking in the bathtub reading (well, trying to read a book). At one point I remembered your testimony about thanksgiving. I started thanking God for everything, and almost immediately, he shut up. I continued praising and then moved into asking God to help me help my husband. I honestly didn't know what to say or even if I should say anything. A few moments later, I heard the printer.

This really touched me. I knew right then and there that my Heavenly Father was listening to me and that he cared about me, and his presence was so real. I am still somewhat amazed how thanksgiving makes the enemy flee and draws one so close to God.

Also, while on the subject of prayer I was listening to Dr. David Jeremiah on the National Day of Prayer and he said something that really struck me. He said something like, "God doesn't need our prayer to make things happen. He's all powerful and can do anything that we could come up with, but He wants someone to ask him." He said it better, but it has challenged me to pray more.

Talk to you later,

R---

It wasn't long before this young mother was

sharing the Thankful Principle with others and continuing to apply it in her own life. After this experience, I began to realize how much the testimony was continuing to build when I shared my story with others and saw them applying it in their own lives and seeing results. I began looking for opportunities to share my testimony with others who were feeling like victims of circumstances, too.

CHAPTER ELEVEN
MISSION TRIP PLANS

In JANUARY OF 2013, both Jacob and Laura were looking into going on a mission trip to Nicaragua with a group from church. While sitting through an information session, they each separately got the idea that if they were going to spend the required funds on a mission trip, perhaps they could go instead to South Africa and be part of my brother's ministry for a similar amount of money. My brother, Chuck, went to the mission field of South Africa in 1991, and although my parents had been there on ministry trips, no one else in our family had ever been there to visit. My children were fond of their uncle and his wife, Sanet, and their children, Taliah (13) and Benjamin (9), so going to South Africa on a mission trip would be an opportunity to serve God and spend time with family.

Laura brought up the idea to me first. I began looking into costs for airline tickets and was surprised to find that if we went at the end of the spring semester in May and flew out of Chicago, we could get roundtrip tickets to Johannesburg for less than $1,000. I had expected the prices to be much higher, so when I found such a reasonable rate, I was hopeful that we could work things out to go. Excited about the prospect of going, I called Chuck and Sanet to find out if the date range would work for them. They told us that they would make it work.

Laura, Jacob, and I all made plans to go, and we were also able to add Jacob's girlfriend, Emily, to our team. The young adults, who were all in college, had enough savings to pay for their tickets. By faith, I trusted and thanked God for the needed funds for my ticket. I knew God had put it in my heart to go, and he would work out the financing for my trip, even though it wasn't necessarily in the family budget. Right on time, God brought extra tutoring and substitute teaching work my way, and he even worked it out for me to sell part of my timeshare vacation points to book someone an affordable honeymoon. Not only did these things provide enough funds for my ticket, but they also helped supply some needed funds for a couple of projects in South Africa. While there, we hoped to help a family of ten to start building a room addition, and we also planned to do some work with local children.

Over a decade earlier, God had already begun preparing my heart to go on a mission trip to South Africa, but at the time, I was busy raising my young family and didn't picture myself going right away. Through the years, it became more of a desire of my heart to go someday. When I would think about it, I knew that "one day" God would give me the opportunity to go and minister in South Africa, and I was looking forward to it. When Laura brought up the idea of the trip, the timing seemed right, and God was already paving the way and preparing our hearts to go. For several months, I continued to thank God for providing for all of our needs to enable us to go and was rejoicing and often marveling over the way God worked out the fine details.

Since we had to change planes in Amsterdam, I was tickled that the Lord helped me to find a way to get to spend one night there without adding to the cost of our tickets. It was a small desire of my heart to see Europe again, since I had spent three years of my childhood in Germany and had fond memories of our family vacation trips to the Netherlands. Consequently, I was excited to share this experience with my children.

Although God worked out the financial needs, I was tested a time or two. When a subbing assignment was unexpectedly taken away, which meant the loss of a few hundred dollars that I had been expecting to use towards the trip, God did not let me stay angry or bitter about it. It wasn't easy, but I began thanking God for the situation, instead of continuing to be frustrated. As it turned out, I was just getting over an illness at the time that I would have had that subbing assignment, so it was a good thing I wasn't responsible for those classes. Later, I was assigned a more desirable subbing opportunity that more than made up for the other loss.

Although Danielle wasn't joining us on the trip, God used her to find some excellent winter clearance deals on children's clothing that we were able to take on our trip for needy children. They pretty much filled an entire large suitcase, and I managed to fill a second large suitcase with candy and an assortment of prizes and other useful items that we planned to give away on our trip. I was pleased that Danielle had a desire to help and had generously donated a portion of the items.

I had asked Laura, Jacob, and Emily to read certain Christian books and scripture passages to prepare our hearts for ministry, and they did honor my request. We were all full of joy and happy anticipation as the date of our departure drew near. As I was praying about our trip, I began asking for God to give us people to minister to or share our faith with on the airplanes and everywhere else we went. Our desire was to be a blessing to everyone we encountered.

CHAPTER TWELVE
OUR ADVENTURE BEGINS

MOTHER'S DAY 2013 was supposed to be the day Jacob graduated with his undergraduate degree from the I.U.P.U.I. campus in Indianapolis. He opted to skip the boring graduation ceremony to enable us to leave on our adventure a day sooner. Since he was receiving his B.A. degree in International Studies, it seemed appropriate to be leaving on a trip abroad instead of sitting through commencement. When we pulled out of our driveway to head to Chicago, it was a miracle that Jacob, Laura, Emily, Dave, and I could all fit inside my husband's sedan.

In addition to five people squeezed into the car, we had also managed to load four large suitcases, four smaller suitcases, a backpack, tote bags, and a few other personal items crammed all around us in the car. We felt like a can of sardines, and it was definitely an uncomfortable, difficult ride to the airport in Chicago, as we rode awkwardly draped around our luggage items. With traffic jams slowing down our progress when we got to the city, everyone was feeling a little edgy, but we were thankful that we had left a bit early to head to the airport and arrived there well before our time of departure.

Laura treated me to a Mother's Day salad at the airport, while we waited to board the plane. Our first leg of the journey was a flight from Chicago to Atlanta, and we had been assigned three seats together and one across the aisle. The three young adults sat together, and I opted to take the single seat nearby. Since I had prayed for the right seatmates on our flights, I could hardly wait to see who was going to sit next to me. As passengers continued boarding, I was watching and waiting for my appointed seatmate. When the influx of passengers seemed to stop, it appeared that the seat next to me might remain empty. I was beginning to feel a strong sense of disappointment.

As I was sitting there watching the steady stream of new passengers dwindling down, I thought to myself somewhat indignantly, "Really? Really, God? After I prayed for the right seatmate, you're going to let the seat next to me stay empty?" I was baffled because I had been so sure that God was going to send someone for me to talk to on each leg of the journey, and I was beginning to feel a bit let down. I probably seemed like a petulant child, and God was probably chuckling and thinking, "O ye of little faith."

Within moments, I spotted a young Indian man making his way down the aisle. As he edged closer, it became clear that God was sending me a seatmate after all. My heart rejoiced, and I felt instantly convicted about the fact that I had doubted God a few moments earlier. "Please forgive me, Lord," I said sheepishly in a quiet prayer.

I introduced myself to the young man in his mid-twenties, and I learned that he had lived in America for about three years and was living in Atlanta. Somehow in our conversation, I mentioned the fact that I used to write for an educational poster company for seventeen years and still had many posters displayed in schools everywhere, including some posters that were still on the market. I happened to quote one of my favorites to him: "Stand up for what is right, even if you're standing alone." I shared the fact that it is the one poster editorial piece that I am most proud of writing and mentioned how I try to live it daily.

Immediately, my seatmate became excited and let me know that he had posted that quote on his Facebook page. I gained instant credibility with him, and he was pleased to meet the person behind the quote. We talked about our respective faiths of Christianity and Hindu. I shared my thankful testimony with him, how God brought me my husband, and more. I let him know that it was no accident that he and I had ended up as seatmates, but that I had prayed and asked God to send the right person. He had enjoyed our conversation and agreed that it was not a mere coincidence, and before we got off the plane, he asked about adding me on Facebook and immediately sent me a friend request.

As I disembarked from the plane, I thought to myself, "Wow!" This first leg of our journey generated more excitement about the adventures ahead. My heart was overflowing, and I prayed, "Thank you, Lord, for answered prayer and for being faithful in the choosing of my seatmate. Forgive me for ever doubting."

I felt extremely blessed as I walked off the plane with my children and Emily. Time and again, God is faithful and always does even more than we can ever ask or think. I had greater confidence that more good things were to follow.

Chapter Thirteen
Amsterdam

OUR SECOND FLIGHT was a red-eye from Atlanta to Amsterdam, and the four of us shared a center row together. In the last hour of our flight, I did engage in some friendly conversation with some Dutch travelers across the aisle. I told them about our plans for the mission trip to South Africa, but nothing exciting happened on that flight, since we mostly tried to get some sleep. When we arrived in Amsterdam in the early afternoon, we were delighted to see a few tulips in bloom and quickly made our way to the hotel shuttle bus.

Originally, I had planned to spend the afternoon and evening exploring Amsterdam, since our stay would be slightly less than twenty-four hours. However, Jacob was so exhausted from the overnight flight, he didn't want to leave the hotel. I didn't feel it would be as safe for the rest of us to explore without him, and I told him how I felt. I was not happy about Jacob's desire to stay put, after the fact that I had gone to the extra trouble and expense of reserving two hotel rooms for one night in order for us to see a bit of Amsterdam. I tried to cajole him into cooperating with me and was starting to get a bit ticked off with his stubborn attitude.

When I couldn't get anywhere with my son by reasoning with him on my own, I resorted to quietly thanking God that he would work things out in a manner that was agreeable to all. At least thanking God helped me to feel calmer about the situation, and we were able to eventually come to some sort of resolution. After the compromise of a short nap for Jacob, while the rest of us got showers and cleaned up, we all took the shuttle back to the airport and caught a train into the heart of downtown Amsterdam. I was pleased that Jacob had lost the negative attitude and was agreeable to our going out for at least a few hours of sightseeing. I thanked God for another answered prayer and was again reminded that thanking God could change me, the situation, or both.

When we walked out of the train station in the heart of Amsterdam, one of the first things we spotted was a building that had a "Jesus Loves You" sign in large letters hung near the top of the building. It turned out to be the Youth With A Mission (YWAM) building, a place my brother Chuck had spent time at in 1982 on a summer mission trip during his college days. This brought to mind a story that Chuck had shared with me upon his return.

I related the story to my kids and Emily of a night that Chuck was out in the Red Light District of Amsterdam. Chuck had been out jogging late at night, when a drunken man threatened to beat him up. Just prior to this incident, my brother had been out on an evening run and praying that God would help people to notice something different about him that would help them to see that he was a

Christian. The drunken man had assumed that because Chuck was wearing a red bandana when he was out jogging that night, he must have been the same guy who had beaten up the man's brother earlier in the evening. The victim had described his assailant as an English-speaking person who was wearing a red bandana; consequently, the drunk made the accusation. Although Chuck told him that he was not the person who had harmed the brother, the man did not immediately believe Chuck.

When the man began waving a broken off chair leg and making threats about beating up my brother, Chuck immediately replied, "In the name of Jesus, you can't harm me because I'm a man of God!" At first, Chuck was scared when he said it, but remembering the testimony of a missionary who had done that, he kept repeating it over and over again. After saying it several times, Chuck began to believe it, too, and this gave him a new confidence each time he repeated the statement.

Suddenly, the guy stopped and said menacingly, "I have a knife in my back pocket. I don't want to have to use it."

Chuck thought it was strange for the man to say that and realized that something must have been preventing the guy from striking him with the chair leg. With greater confidence he replied boldly, "In the name of Jesus, you can't harm me because I'm a man of God!"

Finally, the man stopped and said, "Well, if you really are innocent, you won't mind going to the police station and answering some questions."

Chuck agreed to go, but on the way, the man paused and asked, "Are you REALLY a man of God?"

Chuck responded that he really was a man of God.

"I believe you. At first I did not believe you," replied the man, "but then something in your voice let me know that you really are a man of God."

The two men then sat down on the curb, and Chuck shared about his faith and what it meant to be a man of God. Although the man did not make a decision to come to Christ that night, Chuck planted some spiritual seeds and walked away unharmed.

Even though it was over thirty years later, it was fun to walk the streets of Amsterdam with my children and remember Chuck's amazing story of God's protection. We returned to the hotel that evening and turned in early. How good it was to sleep in a bed that night after the red-eye flight the evening before. We had a plane to catch for Johannesburg, South Africa, in the morning and were feeling blessed to be closer to our destination.

CHAPTER FOURTEEN
FIRST IMPRESSIONS

OUR FLIGHT TO JOHANNESBURG was a lengthy one of nearly eleven hours, and since my seatmate was Laura, I really didn't have much opportunity to converse with strangers. When we arrived later in the evening, the combination of warm temperatures in the airport and the fact that we were both wearing our jackets had apparently raised my body temperature and Laura's. Some sort of device detected that fact, so Laura and I had to be taken out of the passport line for official entry into the country. I was a little concerned, and the woman explained that they needed to take our temperatures and make sure we weren't bringing some sort of illness into the country.

I began quietly thanking God for the situation and believed it would work out without any major delays. Fortunately, we were fine and were allowed to proceed into the country without any further problems. Chuck's family of four greeted us with smiles and hugs outside of customs. They came with their two vehicles in order to carry all of our baggage and to transport all of us back to their home in Pretoria, the administrative capital of

South Africa. It was a happy reunion, filled with lots of joy and excitement, so we stayed up late talking when we got to the house. Chuck and Sanet had planned a full schedule of activities during our stay, and we were eager to begin the work we had come to do.

One blessing for our stay was the fact that Sanet was going to be off from work during the majority of our time in Pretoria. In Sanet's medical job at a nearby hospital, she wasn't supposed to be able to take off from work at that particular time, but the cardiologist she worked with had uncharacteristically planned to attend a weeklong conference during a portion of our stay. In all of her years of working there, that had never happened, but God worked it out for Sanet to have a little more than a full week off during our stay. This enabled her to join in some of our activities and to also provide some of the needed transportation for our mission team of four. We didn't even know this was going to be possible when we planned the trip, so we rejoiced at God's timing of events.

Wednesday, our first morning in South Africa, was basically unstructured to allow for us to get over the jet lag, but we did manage to explore Pretoria for a bit in the afternoon. Chuck also drove us over to the African township of Soshanguve, where he had planted a church in the mid-1990s. Praise Tabernacle East was actually a branch church that was part of a larger African church ministry nearby. My first impression of the township was not exactly what I had expected. Although we saw signs of poverty and homes that included small shacks and some unkempt yards in the township, we also saw modest, sturdier houses that indicated that some families were improving their living quarters and quality of life. I was also struck by the beauty I spied in the midst of some of the worst areas. Within many of the township's gated compounds, I spotted a number of lovely rose bushes growing or patches of green grass surrounded by yards full of reddish dirt.

Chuck also showed us the modest building owned by the church, next door to the Waka Waka Market, a small neighborhood grocery store. We were supposed to be running a math tutoring session at the building that afternoon, but due to a conflict in the schedule, we had to locate a leader in the church to get the word out to cancel the event. Ma Shoba was the first church leader I was able to meet, and I instantly liked her gracious spirit. At the church building, we also met a young lady, Dineo, a university student who helped with the youth ministry and praise team. Slowly, we were getting to know a few of the locals from the township, and they both seemed pleased to meet us.

The next morning, Thursday, I ended up accompanying Chuck to a weekly bible study he led at Lewende Woord, an Afrikaans ministry and bible school. It was fun walking around and meeting some of Chuck's colleagues and introducing myself to them, while he prepared for his lesson that morning. Even in my late forties, I was proud to be Chuck's little sister and was glad for the opportunity to catch a glimpse of his ministry and meet the people he worked with.

Since I knew I would be speaking at Chuck's township church on Sunday morning, I decided to use some of my spare time that morning to work on my message. I went back and read the fourth chapter of Philippians. Even though I had read it many times, I still found that I could be impacted in new ways by the familiar passage. I began taking notes and writing down the insights that I wanted to share.

"Rejoice in the Lord always. I will say it again: Rejoice! Let your gentleness be evident to all. The Lord is near. Do not be anxious about anything, but in every situation, by prayer and petition, with thanksgiving, present your requests to God. And the peace of God, which transcends all understanding, will guard your hearts and your minds in Christ Jesus.

Finally, brothers and sisters, whatever is true, whatever is noble, whatever is right, whatever is pure, whatever is lovely, whatever is admirable—if anything is excellent or praiseworthy—think about such things. Whatever you have learned or received or heard from me, or seen in me—put it into practice. And the God of peace will be with you" (Philippians 4:4-9, NIV).

I began noting the fact that verse four talks about rejoicing in the Lord "always." Because it was so important to his message, Paul repeated the instruction for emphasis. Paul also instructed the church in Philippi to "not be anxious about anything." I began to think about the fact that no matter how big or small the problem, God doesn't want us to worry about it. In "every situation, by prayer and petition, with thanksgiving," we are instructed to present our requests to God. Not only are we promised the peace that "transcends all understanding," but Paul describes that peace as guarding our hearts and minds in Christ Jesus. If we are at peace, our hearts and minds cannot be in turmoil.

I also noticed in verse eight, the instruction to

think about things that are "excellent or praiseworthy." This is great advice because the alternative is to fret or worry. In the book of Psalms, we are advised as follows: *"Refrain from anger and turn from wrath; do not fret—it leads only to evil"* (Psalm 37:8 NIV). By keeping our minds and hearts in Christ Jesus and thinking right thoughts, we are avoiding destructive behavior.

Verse nine would be my challenge to the congregation in my message that Sunday. Paul challenged the church in Philippi to live the things they had received, heard, or seen in him and "put it into practice." Basically, Paul was telling them, "Take my testimony and run with it." I wanted to encourage the church to not only understand the Thankful Principle, but to use it in their daily lives regularly and experience life-changing results, too.

Even after nine years, God was continuing to help me to grow in my understanding and practice of the Thankful Principle. Instead of merely thanking God regularly during trying times, God was working on my heart to make thankfulness a daily habit for all situations, big or small. The desire to share the message was growing more fervently in my heart, and I felt this was a major part of God's purpose and plan for the mission trip. I was looking forward to sharing this message with Chuck's church in just a few days because I believed it would be a blessing to those who heard it.

In the afternoon, Chuck took our missions team back to Soshanguve, where we met with a husband, wife, and the younger half of their family of eight children. Although the wife and children were attending Chuck's church, the husband was part of a religious group that included elements of

Christianity and ancestral worship. We had planned to help the couple to build a room addition, since they were currently living in a crowded, one room shack that was made of corrugated iron. As it turned out, it was decided that the corrugated iron addition would have issues with water leakage, so it wasn't entirely a desirable type of a shelter to construct. The husband had bigger and better plans, which included him building a house made of bricks and doing the majority of the work himself. With the assistance of his wife, he dug a trench for the foundation of a modest, four-room brick house, which would be much sturdier. They had already made some of the bricks themselves and had also received leftover bricks from a recent building project from Chuck's church. We had brought funds that we had raised and some that had been given to us, so we used them to buy other needed supplies, such as gravel, sand, cement, and other building materials. At least we could get the project started while we were there and continue to send funds after we returned home. The couple was also using a portion of their limited income towards the building materials.

That afternoon, Laura, Jacob, and Emily played with the four younger children and a neighbor girl at the building site that was located in the same compound as the family's current one-room home. The children were delighted with the small toys and treats that we had brought along, and they were also fascinated with having their pictures taken and viewing the results of the still photos and videos. As much as possible, I tried to visit with the wife, who was somewhat limited in her English skills, but we somehow found a way to communicate. Her husband was more fluent in English, but he and

Chuck were busy arranging for some of the building supplies.

When a load of gravel had been dumped outside of the gate of the family's compound, we used shovels and wheel barrows that the family owned or had borrowed from neighbors and began moving the small mound of gravel inside the chain-link fence to keep the building materials safe from theft. It was quite a sight to the neighbors to see a group of five Americans doing manual labor in the neighborhood. Several made a point of walking by to get a closer look at the foreigners or to speak to us briefly. A young man came up and asked my brother for work, but he was surprised to learn that we were the volunteers and were working for the homeowner. Our assistance that day was primarily in terms of moral support more than providing much in the way of physical labor, although I did get a blister from shoveling. We mainly wanted the family to know that we were concerned for them and wanted to assist. Our symbolic gesture did not go unnoticed by the family we were helping, especially the husband. His hard work and determination to complete the project was impressive, since he could easily do twice the work of any one of us.

It touched me that we would be instrumental in dramatically changing the lives of this large family's living situation. I considered how easily we took things for granted, such as a nice home, abundant food, flushing toilets, transportation, and a variety of other luxuries that we look at as necessities that we couldn't live without. My experience in seeing how others lived was beginning to teach me to be thankful for these things and more.

The next day was Friday, and we visited a day

school run by Ma Thoko, a dear lady from the church. It was essentially a small daycare center for local children in the township, and the children were so excited to greet the American visitors. Some of the kids were meeting Americans for the first time ever, so it was an exciting event in their young lives. We brought some of the new clothing items to share with the children who were in need of clothes and loved seeing the happy expressions on the faces of the children in their new outfits. The students sang a special song for us, and their teachers had us sign autographs for them to take home that day.

At first, my sister-in-law, the girls, and I were the only ones from our team visiting and playing with the children, but later Chuck and Jacob joined us. At six foot, four inches tall, Jacob was especially impressive to the small kids and was a big hit. He and the little ones showed off their muscles and made fast friends. Later, he lifted some of them up into the air and let them climb on him like a jungle gym. In honor of our visit, the staff at the school made us a thoughtful presentation of the gift of a set of spoons that were decorated with Zulu beading. We were touched by their sweetness and generosity.

As we departed, the children followed us to the gate and seemed sorry to see us leave. They touched our hearts that day. Although we had come with the intention of being blessings and goodwill ambassadors to others wherever we went, we were also the recipients of multiple blessings, too. Our hearts overflowed from the love shown by the children and teachers, and I continued to thank God for these gifts along the journey.

CHAPTER FIFTEEN
THANKFUL LESSONS IN SOSHANGUVE

THE FIRST WEEKEND we were in South Africa, the women on the team accompanied my sister-in-law, Sanet, to Soshanguve, where we attended the monthly women's fellowship meeting on Saturday afternoon. This was our first opportunity to become acquainted with a sizeable group of members from Chuck's congregation, and we also met some Afrikaans friends of Sanet's who were from the Lewende Woord church and had come to help. It was a sunny afternoon, and we met outdoors in the compound area outside of the home of one of the ladies from the church. Many chairs were set up already and some of the ladies brought their own chairs. About thirty or more women came for fellowship that day. Because I was scheduled to lead a math tutoring session at the same time, I went inside one of the smaller homes within the family compound and worked with three teenagers. While Sanet was leading the women's meeting, Laura and Emily had fun doing crafts and playing games with the children of the ladies who were attending the fellowship group.

After the meeting was over, we greeted the ladies, who were eager to welcome us and meet the members of Chuck's extended family. While we were visiting, I spoke again with Ma Thoko. She told me that she had received several phone calls on Friday night from parents who wanted to know why their children were so excited that they couldn't settle down and go to bed that night. Apparently our appearance at her school the previous day had been a success. While we talked that afternoon, Ma Thoko also shared her dream with me of someday opening a day school for children with disabilities. It was a noble goal, and I was even more impressed when I learned that at her current day school, she didn't even take a salary for herself. Because some of the parents were experiencing economic struggles and were not always reliable in paying their bills, Ma Thoko was using the funds that did come in to pay for the expenses of the school and staff salaries first, which didn't leave anything for her personal needs. Her work was a ministry, though, and she did not complain. I was thankful for the opportunity to meet this godly woman, who was an inspiration to me. Instead of complaining about her current situation, she was trying to do even more to be a blessing in her community.

The next morning, we returned to Soshanguve for the Sunday morning church service at Praise Tabernacle East. We brought along many supplies of candy and prizes for an American birthday party that we intended to host that afternoon for the children's ministry of the church. Sanet had made dozens of cupcakes and larger cakes for the occasion. I realized we needed to have some lunch supplies, too, so we quickly stopped by a local grocery store, where I had my first experience in an African store and bought a number of loaves of bread, a large 5 kg roll of lunch meat that I had sliced for the occasion, as well as a few other lunch supplies.

When we arrived at the church, we were treated as honored guests and were greeted with cheers and a small celebration by the members of the congregation, who lined the street to sing to us as one large welcoming committee. They joyously escorted us into the morning church service in true African style with lots of singing and dancing. It was merry and festive, especially since about half of the adult congregation had donned colorful costumes for the occasion to share African culture with us and to educate us about the variety of African people groups that were represented in their congregation. We were treated to a great deal of singing and dancing that morning, and we thoroughly enjoyed it. During the festivities of the morning service, I was presented with a lovely beaded Zulu necklace, bracelet, and headband, which I proudly wore throughout the remainder of the service.

Many were curious to meet the sister and family of Pastor Chuck, and it warmed my heart to see the genuine love and affection of the church members toward my brother. When it was time for the morning message, I was introduced and had my first experience of publicly speaking with an interpreter. Although many in the congregation understood English, the service was also translated into Zulu for those who did not understand English. It was a little challenging to get used to the pacing, but I began to get into a rhythm in sharing the story of my journey into thankfulness.

As I had already come to know some of the people in the township and had seen the present issues of poverty, lack of jobs, and more, I began to recognize just how needed the message of being thankful in the midst of trying circumstances was going to resonate with the people of the church. Except for the sermon that I shared at the women's prison, this was only the second time I had shared the Thankful Principle in a message presented to a congregation, so I was slightly nervous and excited, too.

When I got to the part of the story about Danielle's unexpected pregnancy, I shared that when I first met Eric, he was not a mother's idea of ideal dating material for her daughter. I described the details of the warts and the struggles that I had experienced in Danielle and Eric's rocky relationship over a period of nearly four years. Parents in the congregation could definitely relate to my situation of disappointment in a child's choice in a love interest, and I saw many of the mothers nodding their heads in agreement over my trials during this turbulent period. It was easy for the congregation to agree that my situation had seemed hopeless or frustrating at times; therefore, they were mildly shocked when I stated that my opinion of Eric had vastly improved. I stated, "He's not like that anymore. Miraculously, God has made many positive changes in his life. He is now serving God and becoming a godly man, and I'm pleased to announce that he and my daughter are planning to get married in a couple of months with my husband's and my approval." The congregation clapped and cheered at this news and shared in the joy of our upcoming family nuptials. Everyone loves a story with a happy ending, and I was reminded of

just how far these two had come and was thankful
to God for the positive changes.

At the end of my message, I challenged the
congregation to come before God with thanksgiving
and make their requests known to him. I reminded
them that I was not any more special and that God
was willing to do for them what he had done for me
in my life. I told them that I was expecting to hear
good news from them the following week. I wanted
to hear reports that they had tried it, and it worked
for them, too. I just knew that wonderful
testimonies would be forthcoming. God's word does
not return void, and I was already anticipating in
faith the good reports still to come.

When I had finished my message and sat down,
Pastor Zwane, the associate pastor who had been
my translator that morning, smiled and told the
congregation that I preached "just like Pastor
Chuck." My brother and I had both been heavily
influenced by our father's preaching style, so I took
it as a compliment. Due to my slight nervousness
in speaking that day, I didn't wrap up my sermon
the way I had intended, but God knew just how to
finish the word perfectly. As I was sitting on the
front row and thinking about a few of the things
that I wished I had said, Pastor Zwane summed up
the main points of my sermon and was even more
eloquent in saying what I had intended to say at the
end. He, too, challenged the people to put
thankfulness into practice. I marveled at the
outcome and was thanking God for finishing the
message that day so beautifully, as only he could
do.

CHAPTER SIXTEEN
PRAISE REPORTS

A COUPLE OF DAYS after the Sunday service, our team stopped at a warehouse store to purchase items for the township church and our team's projects. Since I was going to be running a math tutoring session that day in Soshanguve, I decided to purchase some affordable scientific calculators, snacks, pencils, and paper for the kids who would be participating. I initially grabbed eight calculators, but when I thought about the price being so reasonable, I felt inspired to go back and purchase an additional five more.

Afterwards, we stopped by the building site to check on the progress of the house before heading to our math tutoring session. Chuck dropped Laura, Emily and I off at Ma Shoba's house to meet for the math tutoring session, and then he and Jacob assisted with the foundation work at the new house. The students who attended the math session ranged in age from upper elementary to high school, and we had a good time getting to know them. We not only worked on answering mathematics-related questions, but we also spent time getting to know the students and answering their questions about life in America. I was pleased to see that Laura and Emily were natural teachers with the younger children and some of the high school kids made a point of working together and helping each other. Ten of the calculators made it into the hands of the students who needed them that day, and it was a productive help session.

The next night, we attended the weekly cell group meeting in Soshanguve at the home of a local lady from the church named Annah. Because the members of the church knew our team would be coming with Chuck that night, the group had a boost in its regular attendance. People filled almost every square inch of the living room and adjacent dining area, as well as the hallway. A few even stood in the kitchen to listen to our sharing that night. Altogether, we had at least forty-five or more people in attendance, including children.

During the meeting, each person in the room answered the question, "How was your weekend?" Many that had attended Sunday's service mentioned that their weekend was "awesome," and they made positive remarks about the Sunday service. A few others who had not been to church on Sunday reported on being sick or away at a funeral that weekend. Several of them expressed disappointment in having missed the service, especially after hearing favorable reports.

Dineo, the lovely young lady that we met on our first visit to Soshanguve, was interpreting between English and Zulu, so everyone could understand what was being said that night. She mentioned to the group that on the previous Sunday, several people had approached her to ask about my name. Because Marcia (pronounced Mar-shuh) was hard for some of them to remember or pronounce because of the "r" sound, she and a few others had unofficially given me the nickname "Mother Thank You." I was both delighted and honored by the new designation. Mother Thank You had a nice ring to it.

One older South African lady seemed extremely happy and delighted when it was her turn to share. She spoke in Zulu and remarked that she was so excited to "meet Americans" for the first time in her life. I made a comment about the fact that Pastor Chuck is an American, but she shook her head and replied, "He doesn't count. He's one of us!" I was amused at the great esteem she showed my brother.

As the testimonies and sharing continued, my ears perked up when a high school student named Angie quietly shared that she had tried the Thankful Principle and "it worked." She did not explain further. Immediately, I had to inquire for details. I quickly whipped my head around to where she was seated behind me and asked her, "What happened? How did it work?"

Chuck later good naturedly chided me for my rudeness in interrupting, but he told me that those in attendance probably didn't mind my actions, since I was a guest. I was just so excited. I seriously needed to know what had happened and could not wait to find out the particulars.

Angie vaguely shared that she was having some difficulty in her schoolwork and then began thanking God for the situation. Somehow, it made a difference for her and the frustration left. As we went around the room, a few others reported trying the Thankful Principle and how it had worked for them. One young woman had been accused of unplugging a co-worker's computer, and he was angry with her. She was extremely upset, so she went into the bathroom and cried. Remembering my message, she began to thank God for the situation and began to be at peace. The next day when she went to work, her co-workers immediately ushered her into a room with an expensive gift waiting for her. It was a gift from the co-worker who had distressed her the day earlier, and the gesture blessed her. Sam, a teen from the youth group, testified that he had thanked God for not having lunch money one day at his high school, but he ended up with a full plate of food. Dineo reported that a young woman was arguing with her, and when she quietly prayed and thanked God during this negative exchange, the person suddenly stopped arguing with her. A couple of other people also shared testimonies of the Thankful Principle working for them, too.

I was thrilled beyond words, and my heart swelled with gratitude to God for enabling me to hear these testimonies and to rejoice with those who were seeing favorable results. They had received the message and were already putting it into practice in their daily lives. Not only that, but by sharing their stories, they were helping and encouraging others in the group to understand the benefits of exercising the Thankful Principle, too. They no longer had to just take my word on it.

During the meeting, I also shared a brief recap about the passage in the fourth chapter of Philippians to explain the Thankful Principle to those who had missed the Sunday service. I wanted to make sure they understood what all of the excitement was about. Not only was it important for them to learn about the scriptural basis for coming before God with thanksgiving and making their requests known, but I hoped that the mini lesson would serve as a reminder to those who had already heard the message the first time.

Afterwards, while some were enjoying tasty refreshments sent by Sanet, Chuck and I were praying for and ministering to several of the people in attendance with various needs, both physical and spiritual. Later, as I spent some time trying to get better acquainted with people, one lady shared about her need for a job, and another lady shared with me her worries for her son, who had been taken away to a "circumcision school." I had never heard of one, but learned that in Africa, it is a common practice for young men to be suddenly whisked away for several weeks or months to some unknown location, circumcised, and forced to undergo some sort of rite of passage for African males. In America, we would consider that kidnapping and criminal behavior, but I learned that it is very common occurrence there. Just that month, reports had been published that a number of young men in South Africa had died at a circumcision school under unsafe conditions. This mother was worried that her son might have been one of the victims. I prayed and thanked God for her situation and prayed for her son's safe return, and I also prayed that she would be at peace during this difficult time. (I learned a few months later that her son was safely home again and rejoiced for her.)

Two high school girls, Angie and her friend Pretty, spoke to me at the end of the meeting. "Mother Thank You, we're sorry that we missed your math class yesterday." It was the first time someone had addressed me with my new nickname, and it made me smile. I had brought my remaining calculators from the previous day with me and asked them, "Do either of you need a scientific calculator?" They both nodded their heads in agreement, so I pulled out two of my leftover calculators for them and added, "I have just one calculator left. Do you know of any other teen from the church who might need one?" Immediately, they pointed to Sam, the young man who had thanked God for not having lunch money and God had supplied him with food. As it turned out, Sam did need one and was happy to get it. I was pleased that God had led me to purchase exactly the right number of calculators that were needed.

For the rest of the evening, I could hardly contain my joy over the testimonies that had been shared that night. I rejoiced that people were putting the Thankful Principle to work within the first three days of hearing the message. I wanted to jump up and down, shouting, "Praise God! Praise God! Praise God!" God's blessings were heaped up and spilling over, and I thanked him all the way back to Chuck's house that night.

CHAPTER SEVENTEEN
TESTING AND TESTIMONY

As our trip continued into the second week, I found myself even more mindful of my spending habits. I began to see that if I denied myself certain pleasures and souvenirs, I could have more to use towards helping others and meeting small needs before I left. I realized that the funds I had converted to rand and brought with me were limited, so I didn't want to squander them all on things for myself or on gifts to bring home to the U.S. I was already kicking myself for some earlier purchases I had made on the trip. Although I had often prided myself on being a good steward, I realized that there were many areas in my life where I could economize more and have funds left to bless someone else.

On Friday, five days after I had preached on thankfulness in Chuck's church, I had a trial of my own. My summer school class at the college had been cancelled, but I had requested weeks earlier to teach another class that would have fit my schedule and replaced the other class. I had fully expected to be granted that class, since it had not been assigned to another instructor, but the start of the semester was looming with no word given. That morning, I received a reply to my e-mail from my boss, after I had inquired about the assignment of the class. His note started apologetically, and he explained that he thought he had seen all of the scheduling requests. He further shared that through some mix-up, he had not seen my request and had given the class to another instructor the day before. My personal record of teaching fifty-two consecutive semesters had come to a screeching halt.

At first, I was stunned and irritated, as well as disappointed, but then the thought came to me, "Do you really believe what you preached last Sunday? Here is your chance to prove it. Are you going to be thankful in the midst of this trying circumstance, or are you just a hypocrite?" The realization felt like a slap in the face that stung afterwards. Over and over that day, those thoughts ran through my mind.

I didn't want to be a hypocrite, so I decided that I needed to be thankful. It wasn't easy, but I also reminded myself that the other colleague had needed the class, too, since she was in the same boat that I was in with a class that had been cancelled. Although I would miss the income, I knew that God would provide in other ways. It was my first summer off in eighteen years, and I was thankful that I would have time to help Danielle plan her wedding. I prayed, "Thank you, Lord, that you are my provider. Thank you for the extra time off. I trust that you will bring good out of this situation."

I can't say that I was totally at peace, as those ugly thoughts would try to return and frustrate me over the situation. Sometimes I wanted to vent and complain, but when I would realize what was happening, I would begin thanking God again for the situation and for being the solution to the problem. Peace began to follow, and I began to see other silver linings in the forced time off. Besides, I wasn't about to let anger and hurt feelings diminish the last few days of the mission trip.

The next day, Saturday, we returned to Chuck's church for a youth work day. Laura, Jacob, and Emily joined the church youth group in painting the walls of the courtyard at the church building and enjoyed the fellowship. While the youth were horsing around and painting, Sanet was cleaning and organizing inside the building with some of the teens and adults, and I began working with a couple of ladies from the church to make a large fruit salad. The ladies were intrigued with learning how to make a fruit salad, since they had never seen one made before. It seemed strange to me that something as simple as cutting up fruit for a fruit salad was something new to them. We cut up a variety of fruits and placed them in a huge salad bowl. As I was nearly finished, Sanet said something about sugar, and I grabbed a jar and sprinkled half of the container on the fruit salad and placed the finished salad in the refrigerator to chill for a few hours before dinner that evening. Everyone was excited about the evening meal, since our dinner also included a grilled leg of lamb that had been cooking on a spit most of the day. It smelled heavenly, and we were all anxious for a hearty meal.

When dinner was served and most of us were sitting outside eating, Chuck inquired loudly, "Who put salt in the fruit salad?" I was mortified, as I realized that the jar that I assumed had contained sugar was actually a jar of salt. I felt terrible that the lovely fruit salad was ruined. Some of the group ate it anyway, but it tasted awful after soaking up the salt I had poured on hours earlier.

The next morning at church, I made the announcement to the congregation that in America we don't actually put salt on our fruit salad, and I apologized profusely for my error. Everyone had a good chuckle over the matter and all was forgiven. I had been scheduled to speak again that morning, so I started off my message by telling them about my thankful test on Friday in regards to my job and my disappointment in not getting the class.

Prior to leaving for South Africa, I had been informed that I would be speaking both Sunday mornings at Chuck's church in Soshanguve. All along I had planned to share my thankful testimony on the first Sunday, but I was puzzled about what I would speak on the following Sunday. As I prayed that week and contemplated what God would have me to share, I felt led to share my personal testimony with the church.

I began by telling them that I was raised in a Christian home with a father who was an Air Force chaplain. I was five years old when I became a Christian, and I shared about my initial reluctance and experience of being filled by the Holy Spirit at the age of fifteen. I shared various scripture passages that God had used to speak to me at various times in my life and tied them into my message. I talked about how God had led me to the right college, my first teaching job, how he miraculously brought me a Christian husband, and more. Looking back, it was clear to me how the Lord had directed my steps and had used my talents in amazing ways. I had so much to be thankful for, and bringing these stories to my remembrance and sharing them with others filled my heart with gratitude to God.

When I shared the story about starting my first teaching job at a little Christian school in Missouri, I mentioned that my sister had suggested a few months earlier, that she thought I should teach in her home state of Hawaii. At the time, I replied, "Oh, Susan, I could never teach in Hawaii because there are too many cultural differences."

Later, as I thought about what I had said, I felt the Lord gently nudge me with the words, "Marcia, don't you think that if I wanted you to teach there, I could help you overcome the cultural differences?"

Immediately I thought, "God must want me to teach in Hawaii." I had already planned to spend a month there to visit my sister's family, right after I graduated from college. While there, I would plan to look for a teaching job. Prior to going, though, I had interviewed for a teaching job at a Baptist church in the town of Nevada, Missouri. I had honestly felt that I had wasted my time in going to the interview because the pay was low and the responsibilities were numerous. It was essentially a one-room schoolhouse, and I wasn't sure I would like teaching multiple grades or whether I could handle that sort of responsibility.

Although I interviewed for jobs on my vacation, none were opening up for me in Hawaii. In mid-July, the church in Missouri called and offered me their open position while I was still in Hawaii. After praying about it, I felt that God wanted me to accept the job. I realized that God didn't necessarily want me to teach in Hawaii, but he wanted my obedience in going where HE wanted me to go. I needed to be willing to go wherever God led. About a week before returning to my home in Kansas, I went on a few dates with a young man from my sister's church, and I reluctantly left this budding relationship to start my new teaching job thousands of miles away.

With a heavy heart, I began preparing to move my things from my parents' home in Kansas to my modest apartment in Missouri. My heart was still in Hawaii, and I began thinking about the possibility of returning to Hawaii just as soon as I got through the school year that hadn't even begun. In my spare time, I was writing another song, and one night I was playing through the melody and memorizing the lyrics that I thought I was coming up with. As I sang through the lyrics a few times, it suddenly dawned on me that God was speaking to me through the song:

> *I know the secrets of your heart.*
>
> *I know your thoughts.*
>
> *I know each part of you.*
>
> *Your hopes and all your dreams.*
>
> *Your future plans.*
>
> *Your crazy schemes.*
>
> *But can't you see? I want you to be part of me?*
>
> *You can be a living sacrifice.*
>
> *My love will suffice.*
>
> *I'm ready to supply all your needs.*

God was showing me that he needed me to go into my teaching job wholeheartedly. Otherwise, he couldn't use me. I repented and told God that I would go where he wanted me to go and that I would do it without any further reservations. In fact the second half of the song, said just that.

I'll go where you lead me.

I'll go where you need me.

I'll go where you want me to go.

I'll go where you'll use me.

Lord, I'll go 'cause you choose me.

I'll go where you want me to go.

As I shared this story and the other glimpses into my life, I wasn't preaching theology. I was speaking words of encouragement, as I shared my journey of God's faithfulness in my life through my personal testimony. I had told them that even though God guided me to a low-paying teaching job, I could trust that he could supplement my income, which he did through my budding success in freelance writing projects. My love story gave single people hope that even if God hides someone away in a small town for two years with no one to date, he can still bring a Christian mate at just the right time. I shared how God used an unpleasant teaching experience with high school students to provide inspiration for motivational poster quotes that would resonate with teachers and be read by millions. Every story demonstrated the faithfulness of God.

Even though we came from different cultures, my stories were ones the congregation could relate to and find uplifting. At the end of the service, Pastor Zwane gave an invitation to receive Christ. Seven adults came forward for a time of prayer for salvation. We rejoiced. I was also asked to pray for a woman who was experiencing a migraine headache, and she immediately felt relief from the pain.

After the service, we took pictures and shared final hugs with our friends at the church. It was hard saying good-bye to everyone in Soshanguve, as it had been a sweet time of fellowship during our visit. When I left, I felt so joyful and thankful for God's faithfulness and goodness, not only for that morning, but for his blessings throughout the entire trip. In sharing the morning message, I was once again reminded of how God's presence had consistently been with me throughout my entire life. I felt so appreciative of the many times God had nudged me and taught me how to trust in him over and over again.

Although we sometimes fail to remember all the many blessings that God has done for us, it is a beautiful thing to revisit the past experiences of God's grace in our lives and to share them with others. Teaching and encouraging others through the word of our testimony can be a powerful blessing; however, hearing our testimony through our own lips also brings to mind the grace we have been given and increases our faith, too.

CHAPTER EIGHTEEN
THANKFUL FOR DELAYS

MONDAY, THE DAY AFTER sharing my testimony with the township church, was to be our last in South Africa. All of our team and Chuck's family felt so blessed by our time together, and it seemed that our thirteen-day stay had been the perfect length of time. Having spent so many years apart from my brother and only seeing him for brief visits every few years, it was meaningful to me to really get to know Chuck with the luxury of extended time. Getting to see him in his place of ministry was another desire of my heart fulfilled, and I was glad that when I returned home, I would be able to picture him and his family in those settings.

Jacob, Emily, Laura, and I had all felt a deep love for the people of South Africa during our time together, and we felt greatly changed by our experiences there. We were heading home with full hearts that night. After a lovely family dinner, Chuck's family dropped us off at the Johannesburg airport with a quick exchange of final hugs and a few last minute pictures. We thanked them for their hospitality and eagerly looked forward to returning home.

While checking in for our 9:15 p.m. flight, we were notified that our plane that was supposed to fly us to Amsterdam had been delayed by several hours. In addition, we would be missing our connecting flight from Amsterdam to Chicago and were going to be rerouted through Detroit to Chicago and arrive late in the evening, instead of the early afternoon. Immediately, I began thanking God for the situation.

I had already felt sorry about the fact that Dave had to drive all the way to Chicago to pick us up and miss a day of work to do so. The thought of him having to pick us up late at night and then enduring a four-hour drive home concerned me a bit. Then an idea popped into my head. Since we were being rerouted to Detroit, perhaps the airline would allow us to fly straight to Indianapolis from Detroit, instead of sending us to Chicago. It probably wouldn't make any difference to them, and it would be a tremendous blessing for us. I was excited by the possibility and was thanking God in advance that he was going to work everything together for the good.

I had plenty of time to thank God, since the slow-moving line at the window I had been sent to was making little progress in helping the people ahead of me. I just knew that God was going to work things out to our advantage. I kept praying quietly and thanking God that he would work out the details for us to catch a flight to our home airport in Indianapolis without incurring any additional cost. When it was my turn at the customer service window, I explained my request, and within minutes, we were scheduled on a connecting flight from Detroit to Indianapolis for no extra charge.

I was rejoicing and sharing our good news with

Laura, Jacob, and Emily, as well as others in the airport. Since I had spent or given away almost all of my rand, I was relieved when we were given vouchers from the airline for food and beverage expenses at the airport. We enjoyed the free treats at a couple of airport restaurants, and God even blessed me with the free use of a phone in one of the restaurants to call Chuck and inform him of the changes in the itinerary. Chuck was thanking God along with us and passed the news on to my husband, who was more than happy to be able to go to work the next day and pick us up that evening at our local airport.

Along the journey home, I shared stories of our trip with fellow travelers and the testimony of the Thankful Principle. I eagerly shared with anyone who would listen about how God was able to route us directly to Indianapolis. I felt blessed all the way home.

CHAPTER NINETEEN
ENCOURAGING WORDS

AFTER OUR RETURN HOME, I was excitedly telling friends, family, and fellow church members about the team's adventures in South Africa. I found myself looking for more opportunities to share the Thankful Principle. As I related the stories from our trip, including the great reports from those who had tried the Thankful Principle and shared about it in the cell group meeting, I would grow excited all over again about the need to share my testimony with others. However, God also used the comments of a new Facebook friend to ignite the fire of spreading this message further.

Angie, the young lady I had spoken with at Annah's cell group meeting, had sent me a friend request on Facebook after I returned home, as did several other young adults and teens from Chuck's church. Angie, age eighteen, was the first one at the cell meeting to testify about trying the Thankful Principle and that it had worked for her.

About two weeks after I returned home, she sent me a Facebook message one morning that started an online chat conversation. I had to get used to Angie's way of writing in a sort of shorthand texting style, since she sent her Facebook messages on a cell phone. (Note: I have translated her original messages into complete words and sentences to make it easier to follow the conversation.)

Angie greeted me that morning by saying, "Hey, Mother Thank You! How's America?"

I smiled at seeing her use my new nickname, as I sat at my computer and responded: "Things are beautiful here —getting ready for summer weather. Trees and grass are all green, flowers are blooming. I'm staying busy trying to get my daughter's wedding planned. Danielle and Eric are getting married July 14th. Have you been practicing the 'Thankful Principle' lately?"

"Yep, it works always, especially now that I am writing exams."

"Glad to hear you are using it. The more I remind myself to do it, the more peaceful and content I am with my life."

"My life has changed after meeting you. Really. You are a blessing. That's why you are blessed."

"Well, thanks. You and your church are a blessing to me. I'm so glad I was able to come and meet everyone. God told me about 10-11 years ago that I would get to come one day. Before that, I had never had a particular desire to come to Africa. I had nothing against Africa, but it just wasn't a place I ever expected to visit."

"Yep, you changed lives. Believe me."

"Well, it was only the Lord's doing. On my own, I can't do anything."

"I miss you already," Angie remarked.

"You made my day today! Thanks!"

"Same here. You reminded me to always thank God. I am going through a rough patch. I believe God made you to talk to me to help."

"Well, I'm glad it has helped you and others. That testimony changed my own life and it is changing the lives of others. Now when it begins to work for you, then you can share with others your own personal testimony of God's faithfulness, and you will in turn bless others and change their lives."

"Yep. I am grateful."

"When we can share God's faithfulness with others, it's not just preaching scriptures. It's showing others the reality of God and the personal relationship they can have."

"Exactly. I was telling this other guy in my class how important it is to thank and worship God. Some people don't really believe."

"Pastor Chuck many years ago met a world famous evangelist who had much success in winning Muslims in Africa to Christ. Chuck asked him why he was successful where many others had failed. He told him that he showed the people a living God and added, 'Anyone will trade a dead God for a living God.' Keep sharing your faith with others and your personal testimony. You never know how God will use it."

"Yes, I've helped a few by sharing, thanks to you."

"Keep it going and keep me posted on your future endeavors. Love to you and the others back in Soshanguve. Depending on my next teaching job, I hope to be back in a year or two."

"I hope so, too. I'll keep you posted, and I hope I can be able to talk over my challenges with you."

Unbeknownst to Angie, she had greatly encouraged me. With God's help, I had been a part of changing lives in South Africa. God was continuing to spread the message of thankfulness through people who had been touched by my testimony. I began to see the bigger picture in God's plan for my visit to South Africa. My story had stirred something in the hearts of the people, and God was using it to change lives. For the first time, I began to see myself as a missionary, instead of just a goodwill ambassador.

Over and over, I pondered Angie's words, "You changed lives. Believe me." It touched my heart and made me even more determined to share with others. More and more, I was spurred to begin looking for opportunities in conversations to share this good news. I spoke to all sorts of people, acquaintances and strangers alike. No place was off limits. I shared in the grocery store, the post office, the bank, at church, on Facebook, in restaurants and at work.

Most everywhere, people were receptive to my encouragement towards thankful living. Some even responded that they would try it, too. I had good news to share, and I couldn't keep it to myself.

CHAPTER TWENTY
WEDDING STRESS

THE SIX WEEKS WE HAD to plan Danielle's wedding, after our return from Africa, were sometimes stressful. I had to handle much of the planning and details, since Danielle was still juggling full-time work and an active three-year-old. We spent time together regularly and worked on getting the invitations, picking out bridesmaid outfits, planning a bridal shower, and putting together a reception. My being off from teaching for the summer gave me free time to help, but it was also pinching the family budget. I thanked God for these blessings and inconveniences and kept trusting that he would bring the right job for me. I thanked God that he was going to make the wedding affordable, too, since we were running on a tight budget.

One evening, I offended Danielle. I had been watching Chloe that day and had been short-tempered with her on the phone when she had called to check on our plans earlier in the day. She had interrupted a nap or something, so I was a bit irritated at the time. When she came by that evening to pick Chloe up, she let me know that I had responded badly on the phone, and she loaded Chloe in the car and left angrily. I had tried to apologize for my part in the flare-up, but she wouldn't sit down and talk to me before leaving. This made me angry, since I would much rather work things out with someone immediately, instead of letting things go for hours or days. I deserved her initial anger, but I was not pleased that we couldn't make peace.

My father once told my husband during our engagement, "Marcia has a short fuse, but she is quick to forgive." At times this was still true. I was very hurt by Danielle's decision to avoid talking with me that evening. I had spent countless hours and energy focused on helping her plan her wedding, and I didn't much appreciate the way I was being treated.

I sent her a long text. I told her how I was feeling unappreciated while working hard on the wedding details, and I threw in the "after all I've done for you" line and added something about her acting like an ungrateful daughter. After I had gotten that off of my chest, I decided I should pray about the matter. A short while later, I began thanking God for Danielle's "crummy attitude." I asked God to forgive me, to show her my true intentions, and to help her to make peace with me.

When Danielle got home, she sent an apologetic text in reply. I knew God had resolved this because I had turned the situation over to him. As I was thinking about our dramatic evening, I sent Danielle another text and said, "I was thanking God earlier for your crummy attitude, and I was amused when it suddenly occurred to me that you were probably thanking God for my crummy attitude, too."

Danielle immediately replied, "All the way home!" She added a smiley face to her text, which made me laugh. I knew all was well between us again.

I deserved that parting shot from her, but it truly blessed me to know that she was using thankfulness as a means of dealing with her problems, too, even though I was the root cause of that particular problem that day. I loved seeing the work God was doing in the life of my precious daughter. She had grown and matured so much in the nine years that had passed since I had first started thanking God in the midst of trying circumstances.

Over the next few weeks, all of the wedding plans came together, and I was amazed at how far the wedding budget stretched. God provided free and discounted items, volunteers who willingly helped with the reception and photography, and an affordable venue in a scenic park setting. I was actually able to enjoy the experience and spend time with my visiting family members and friends without feeling too overwhelmed. I felt blessed more than stressed. Thanking God throughout the planning and preparation period certainly made a difference. On July 14, 2013, Danielle and Eric had a lovely, sunny wedding day, and it was a beautiful and joyous occasion. Three-year-old Chloe, who served as the flower girl, considered the event her wedding, too, for she believed that she and Mommy were marrying Daddy.

I thought about how far this young couple had come over the past four years and thanked God for the significant changes that had brought them to this place of commitment in their relationship. It was the right time for them to marry and continue their journey together, and I thanked God that

Chloe had an intact family. My mother's heart was overflowing with gratitude to God.

CHAPTER TWENTY-ONE
SUMMER SHARING

OVER THE SUMMER MONTHS, Angie and I would have online chats regularly, and I was able to encourage and pray for her needs, as she launched into her final semester of high school. She was receptive to my motherly advice and would send me notes fairly regularly, unless she was bogged down with schoolwork. I also began getting to know a few of my other South African friends through online conversations, too. We often exchanged uplifting words and testimonies. Sam, who had thanked God for not having lunch money, told me that he was still using the Thankful Principle and that it was working in his life regularly. Dineo, my translator at the cell group, was finishing up her coursework at a university and kept in touch. Ellen, a single mother in her early thirties shared in a note that my thankful message was just what she needed to hear at the time she heard me speak in Chuck's church. She went on to correspond with me about a situation she was going through, and my response and advice were confirmations in what God was already showing her. She felt that God had directed her steps in contacting me. This same friend warmed my heart a couple of months later when she asked me, "When are you coming back to South Africa? We miss you like crazy!"

During my devotionals I began reading more of the New Testament writings of Paul. When I came across passages like Philippians 1 and others in which Paul greeted various churches, I could certainly identify with Paul's love for the people he had met on his journeys. *"I thank my God every time I remember you. In all my prayers for all of you, I always pray with joy because of your partnership in the gospel from the first day until now, being confident of this, that he who began a good work in you will carry it on to completion until the day of Christ Jesus"* (Philippians 1:3-6, NIV). A piece of my heart had been left behind, and I yearned to be back once again in their fellowship.

My desire to continue to help fund projects in South Africa was somewhat hampered by my lack of work during the summer months. In April, I had contacted a company that had bought out an educational poster company that I had written editorial for from 1985-2002. Since the new company no longer accepted freelance material, I was unable to continue contributing ideas; however, my posters were literally on the walls of just about every high school and middle school in the country. I used to joke that I had been "read by millions," but nobody knew my name. I had almost given up on ever contacting this company again, but one evening I was showing Danielle which of my posters were still selling and was prompted to try again. This time I wrote a letter to the president of the company through the customer service e-mail, and I pointed out the fact that although I was no longer writing poster editorial, several of my older posters and banners were still on the market, including some that had been selling for twenty years. I suggested that perhaps I was a virtually untapped resource and could be useful to them, possibly in a consulting gig. I ended my letter by asking, "What have you got to lose?"

I was first contacted by someone from the company in May, while I was in South Africa, and the gentleman who contacted me via e-mail encouraged me to give him a call sometime after I returned home, which I did. He asked me to wait a couple of weeks and then continue the conversation. In the interim, he would talk to the president of the company and others on staff about my potential future involvement. When I received the second contact by phone, I was out of town and attending a reunion with college friends. Via e-mail, the gentleman agreed to give me a call on Friday morning or the following Monday, and I was feeling very hopeful that something favorable would come from this. I hoped to know something on Friday because I didn't want to be left hanging for several more days. Since I knew that my time was going to be busy that day exploring Nashville with my girlfriends, I thanked God for the situation and said, "Lord, I could use some encouragement, so would you please let me hear from him this morning?" Within seconds, the phone rang, and it was my contact person.

Eventually, I was given an opportunity to do a consulting project from home, and the timing was perfect. It started just a few days after Danielle's wedding. The job replaced a good portion of the income that had been lost from teaching over the summer, and I thanked God for the open door and for his provision.

In early August, a friend at church had just returned from a mission trip to Nicaragua. We were sharing about our mission trip experiences after church, when I enthusiastically told her about my sermon on the Thankful Principle and the positive results that followed in South Africa. A week later, she grabbed me by the arm and excitedly told me that my thankful testimony had resonated with her and that she had been thanking God all week. She added, "And I have STORIES, but I only have time to tell you one right now." She then went on to relate that her oldest son was going through some legal matter with the mother of his son. The woman was being uncooperative, and it was a stressful situation for the family. On Monday, my friend had begun thanking God for the mother of her grandson and thanking God for the situation. By Friday, her daughter-in-law called her up and said that the boy's mother had miraculously agreed to everything they had asked for. We rejoiced together, and I was thrilled for her family.

The next day, I was feeling happy for a colleague who had just found a permanent faculty position at a community college. Months earlier, I had asked God to give me an encouraging word for him. The scripture God had inspired me to share seemed like an odd passage, but I felt strongly that I was to share it with him. Months had gone by, but nothing was opening up for either of us. In the meantime, my colleague had shared that a chairperson had practically begged him to apply for a full-time position, and he ended up getting hired the same day he interviewed. On the day he started his new job, I took a second look at the passage I had shared with him months earlier. I was amazed at the prophetic nature of the last verse in the scripture passage that God had given me to encourage him: "...*and you will be called Sought After, the City No Longer Deserted*" (Isaiah 62:12, NIV).

That morning I thought a great deal about the fact that I was almost hesitant about sharing that word with my colleague, but God had impressed on my heart that it was the right message to encourage him. This experience confirmed that I had been led by the Lord, but it also challenged me to continue to walk in obedience, even when a message didn't make sense to me. The next day, I wrote a status for my Facebook page that said, "If God gives you a word or scripture passage to share with someone, be obedient. Sometimes, it's just what they need to hear."

A college friend of mine, Fran, commented on my status that day. I hadn't directly heard from her in quite some time, although she had occasionally "liked" a status or photo that I had posted from time to time. We had sort of become distant in our friendship, so it pleased me to see her sweet remark that brought to mind a pleasant memory from our college days. I replied with a quick note to her inbox in which I shared some news with her and also told her the story that was behind my status. This started a fairly lengthy online conversation that helped us to catch up with one another.

One of the things she shared with me really blessed me because I didn't even know she felt this way about me. After I had told her about my recent consulting project with the publishing company, she commented, "You set a great example of persistence. I always found it quite amazing that you knew what you were set out for, and you just went for it, regardless of any obstacles. It's like you didn't see the obstacles, or they were just annoyances to you!"

I was touched by her kind words and thanked her. I went on to tell her about the trip to South Africa and shared the Thankful Principle with her. I added, "I've been a Christian all of my life, but the Thankful Principle turned my life around profoundly. The testimony keeps growing as others report back to me how they applied it and it worked."

Fran replied, "It's powerful, Marcia. It gives hope when you feel like you can't have hope, when you feel judgment, failure, sadness, aloneness, and humiliation —all the damning powers Satan uses to break us down."

Fran and I shared back and forth some more, and we used our conversation to mutually encourage one another. She said that she would try the Thankful Principle and would report back to me how it worked with her and her kids. Then she added, "You shared it with me at the perfect time when I needed to hear it. It was like a confirmation. I recognize that I hold onto the wrongs that have been done to me, and I have to get rid of them. I was just asking God how I can clear my head of these wrongs that I keep holding onto. You gave me the answer. Marcia, you gave me the answer from God! THAT is powerful! It is perfect timing, and it is the same story you will share with so many, but it will impact all of us as it should in God's perfect way. It's your communication of it that is pretty awesome!"

I responded, "Fran, you're making me cry. How beautiful that God's timing is always perfect. I cannot claim credit. It's all him."

Our conversation that night renewed our old

friendship, and I was looking forward to hearing her testimony in applying the Thankful Principle to her life. I had the assurance in my heart that God was going to use it in her life with marvelous results.

Chapter Twenty-two
Seeking God

ALTHOUGH I WAS EXCITED about the receptiveness of others in my sharing of the Thankful Principle, I was also feeling some discouragement in my search for a full-time teaching job. My hours at the college had been drastically reduced as a result of government reforms, and I was getting less than half of the number of hours I generally taught. I continued to trust God that he would provide for our family, whether it be through my getting a full-time job or through Dave's work; however, there were times it was hard not to take the rejection personally.

I had spent countless hours applying to various school corporations, private schools, charter schools, and other employment opportunities. Some online applications took several hours to complete and even included things like a personality profile or involved having to manually enter details that were already on my resume. I had jumped through more hoops than I cared to remember. It was an emotionally draining process, and after months of diligently trying, I had been scheduled for only one sit-down interview for a teaching job. I didn't even wind up getting the job. Another school scheduled me for an interview, but they cancelled it the next day because they had already decided to fill it with another candidate.

At some point, I began thinking, "What's wrong with me?" I felt like an attractive girl who couldn't get a date. I had tons of teaching experience in mathematics, would be a cheap hire (due to the fact that only one year of my experience was in a public school setting), and had glowing recommendations. Why weren't schools interested?

I told Dave that I was going to take a break from job searching because it was becoming too depressing. I figured that I had enough applications on file out there that if someone really wanted to give me a job, it was still possible for me to snag an interview. After five or six months of applying for positions, though, it was obvious to me that there was some reason that a full-time job wasn't coming along at that time, but I just couldn't take the feeling of rejection any longer. Although I was trying to be thankful in the midst of trying circumstances, I still experienced moments when the feelings of rejection would creep in, and I would feel sorry for myself.

Throughout the summer months, the thought had crossed my mind more than once that I might pen my thankfulness testimony and write a book about my journey. I even had the title in mind: **The Thankful Principle**. Although I had not started on the project, the idea lurked in the back of my mind. I shoved those thoughts aside, though, as I began preparing for my fall semester, which included teaching a couple of five-credit algebra classes.

A day after my first day back to teaching my fall classes, I woke up early in the morning and poured my heart out to God. I prayed earnestly about my frustration, "Lord, it's obvious that you are shutting these doors in my face for a reason. What am I supposed to be doing with all of this extra spare time that you've given me?"

Quietly, God spoke in reply, "I told you to write that book. You will begin today, and it will be successful." The message was repeated and was firm and clear, but because of my human nature, like Gideon, I still wanted additional confirmation.

"Lord, can you give me a scripture passage to read this morning?" I asked.

"Psalm 29" came to my mind in reply. I didn't have that one memorized, so I hurried downstairs to open my bible and see what God had to say to me.

"Ascribe to the Lord, you heavenly beings, ascribe to the Lord glory and strength. Ascribe to the Lord the glory due his name" (Psalm 29:1-2, NIV).

The passage itself wasn't particularly speaking to me in its content, but what I did see made me laugh at myself because the first word was "ascribe." In fact, "ascribe" was repeated three times in the first two verses. The message wasn't earth shaking, but it tickled me because when I looked at the word "ascribe," it was also like looking at two words: "a scribe." It seemed as if the Lord was giving me a play on words or sharing an inside joke with me. "A scribe" or "a writer" is what God wanted me to be when he told me to start my book. He had given me the original message loud and clear, but my desire to have an additional confirmation resulted in this amusing exchange. When I did meditate on the words in the first few verses, I was reminded that sharing the Thankful Principle would bring God the "glory due his name."

I was excited to begin the project God had called me to write. The rejection no longer mattered because the jobs that I had applied for weren't God's plan for me. My purpose was growing clear, and I began writing about the Thankful Principle that day.

CHAPTER TWENTY-THREE
A GOOD REPORT

WITHIN TWELVE DAYS, I had already penned 17,000 words of my thankful journey. Reliving these events brought to mind stories I had almost forgotten about, and it stirred in me a greater determination to write them down. God also began opening new doors to share my testimony with others. Whenever God gave me an opportunity, I shared my testimony or a brief word of encouragement, whether it be face-to-face or online. It didn't matter when or where, but I grew more sensitive to the prompting of the Holy Spirit to share. When I casually mentioned to someone the fact that I was writing a book about being thankful in the midst of trying circumstances, I could easily tell them about the story behind the book and share a bit of my testimony.

In early September, I had been wondering how my college friend Fran was doing, since I hadn't really heard from her since I had shared the Thankful Principle with her a few weeks earlier. Fran was busy with her career in commercial real estate, so it wasn't totally unexpected not to hear from her. One night I was surprised to see that she tagged me in her Facebook status post (which I share now with her permission):

"I need to recognize distractions as just that —a distraction. Weigh its importance, put it aside, and remain focused on the good and positives God has before me and blessed me with. It usually works out that by the time I get back to addressing that distraction, it doesn't even require my time and efforts.

Definition of distraction: 'agitation of the mind and/or emotions.' That says it all right there. I would have to say that distractions are not of God.

Quick story: My dear friend, Marcia Day Brown, shared with me her Thankful Principle not a day too soon. On the morning of an investor meeting, I was hit one right after another with crazy negative stuff, and keeping in mind the Thankful Principle, I was able to instantly recognize these as distractions. Rather than become flustered, I was humored. This meant that Satan was trying to defeat me, so this meeting wouldn't go well —which meant to me that this was meant to be a GREAT meeting! So I thanked God for those distractions. I could see them as confirmation that great things were coming from this meeting! And as it turned out, it's one amazing investment for my client! Praise be to God! And thank you, Marcia, for being my friend!"

Of course I was excited and commented on her status, "Fran, I am happy to be your friend and so glad you embraced the Thankful Principle." It blessed me to see her so thrilled about putting it to work in her life and seeing results.

Fran sent a private message to me afterwards:

"Marcia I've been wanting to tell you this —I've been crazy busy. It was so awesome for me to see what was happening and hearing your words. I was

able to totally dismiss the negative and be thankful! I literally laughed out loud thinking in my mind, 'Satan, you thought you'd mess with me, but I've got your number!' LOL! And just like that, those negative attacks just 'poof' went away! So seeing he was on the attack was a confirmation that this was a God thing! Pretty cool. And just think, you were instrumental, designed by God to share that with me! Pretty cool! Gives me goose bumps."

I shared more about my testimony on thankfulness and told Fran about some friends I had worked with on an editing project two years earlier. A husband and wife team were creating a permanent museum exhibit for the company headquarters of a nationally known company. I was editing some of the project to be a second set of eyes for the wife, who was doing all of the writing. Her work involved detailing many decades of the company's history. When my friends participated in project update meetings with company representatives, one gentleman on the team was often negative and problematic. It was as if he wanted to be hard to please, even though this couple had done amazing and creative work on the project. I shared the Thankful Principle on the phone with the wife, and she told me that she was going to try it. She began thanking God for this difficult person and for the problems he was creating. She began thanking God for being the answer to the problems. Amazingly, things changed after she began turning things over to God and thanking him for the situation. She told me that it was like a switch had flipped, and instead of being their adversary, the man became their advocate throughout much of the final stages of the project. Consequently, my friends were able to complete the project successfully without the continued roadblocks. They were thrilled.

I then told Fran about God telling me to write this book and about the progress that I had already made in the first four weeks. By then, I had completed more than half of the book.

She enthusiastically replied, "I'm so excited for you and for your book! Many great things and miracles will come as a result of it. And how awesome is it that God chose you to pen it to paper!"

"Paul penned it first, but I am humbled that God is using me to share it today. I am getting more and more excited about this," I responded.

We talked about other things, such as our kids and their lives, as well as our college days. Later that evening, Fran sent this note: "Scripture God had me read just now for you: 'Finally, my brethren, rejoice in the Lord. To write the same things again is no trouble to me, and it is a safeguard for you,' (Philippians 3:1 NAS). You mentioned earlier Paul penned it first —your book is a safeguard for all who read it."

Pleased by her words, I replied, "Thanks so much for the encouragement. You are a blessing."

The next morning, I chatted online with Fran to further discuss her initial Facebook post about using the Thankful Principle.

I started the conversation by saying to Fran, "I like the take you have on it (the Thankful Principle) about the distractions. I have recognized when Satan is trying to steal my joy in a situation or promote negativity. However, your interpretation and application for you was interesting to me. Thanks for sharing the verse last night, and I am planning to go back and read the passages on rejoicing."

"Marcia, it was so clear for me that morning. It was crazy. That's why I found it amusing. It literally made me laugh. I would not have been so keen on it and certainly would have had a defeated attitude, if you hadn't shared that with me."

"Was it the next day or a few days after we had chatted?" I asked.

"It was the Friday after you shared it with me," Fran replied, which meant it was three days after I had shared the Thankful Principle with her.

"So that meant you had a few days to 'practice,'" I added light-heartedly.

Fran explained eloquently, "Each attack was literally to affect me emotionally, yet really had no bearing on my life. Crazy. They were just little things to upset me, and since I faced them like I did, they literally vanished! That's how I was able to identify them as distractions. Yesterday was the true identifier because one of the same distractions came rearing its ugly head again, and because I had put it aside previously, I had the time to see it for what it really was —a distraction in my life that was NOT of God and only there to steal my joy away. The Thankful Principle essentially keeps you rightly focused and removes the rose-colored glasses or foggy glasses and clears the way. You can call it practice, but I call it getting my mind right by being thankful. Rather than thinking the negative, I was replacing it with being thankful even for the 'painful' or 'ugly' things. The Thankful Principle gets your mind right, which gets your life right."

I responded, "It has taken me a long while for this to become more of a natural reaction. It's very easy to focus on the negatives first or feel the victim or think the worst in a situation. That's why I can now rejoice that my hours were cut at work, thanks to the healthcare reforms. I can rejoice about not getting job interviews. I can thank God that he is in control, he is our provider, and I am to just trust him."

Fran added, "It's almost like when you decide you're going to replace your bad habit of not eating right and working out. You replace the bad habits with good habits. This is replacing the bad thoughts or the negative past with thankful thoughts. Being thankful in all things just puts you right. Great message, Marcia."

We shared a bit more that morning, and then she added, "This has been a breakthrough for me in a very difficult area of my life, and come to find out, there are so many that are in the same place I've been."

Over the next few weeks, Fran continued to encourage me in the writing of this book and even told me that I could share her story. She mentioned that she hoped it would be an encouragement to others. The following month she reported that exercising thankfulness had pulled her out of a dark hole that she had been in for a while and that things were continuing to get better in her life.

It was wonderful to see Fran's testimony unfolding in such a marvelous way. I thanked God and rejoiced with her.

CHAPTER TWENTY-FOUR
THANKFUL MOMENTS

ABOUT THREE WEEKS into my semester, I had several opportunities in a single day to share the Thankful Principle. After my morning class, I went to a local grocery store and happened to speak with a woman who was the manager. I had told her about South Africa and had shared my thankful testimony with her a few weeks earlier, so when I saw her again, I mentioned to her that I had begun writing my thankful book. She was pleased and began sharing with me her concerns about her future and what she wanted to do with the rest of her life, and I was able to share some encouragement and insights with her.

After class that evening, I had an uplifting conversation about the Thankful Principle with a student and then another similar conversation with a security guard at the college. Consequently, I was still at work about an hour after I would have normally gone home. As I was getting ready to finally leave, another security guard walked in with an automatic car starter that needed to be recharged.

Apparently someone needed a jumpstart, but the

machine wasn't working. I offered the use of my car and jumper cables to help out a stranded student. When I got outside, there were two ladies standing by the vehicle. The security guard and I tried to get the other vehicle started with my cables, while the two classmates waited and watched. With the engine running, I sat in my car and began praying and thanking God for the situation and thanking God that he was going to get the other car started. I felt sure that God would answer my prayer and quickly start the car, so I was surprised that it didn't seem to be working right away. After trying several times, it appeared the car just wouldn't start. I began thinking that perhaps I was supposed to give the women a ride home. Maybe the reason the car wasn't starting was because God wanted me to share the Thankful Principle with them.

When the lady who owned the car opted to remain with her vehicle and wait for her husband, I offered to give her classmate a ride home. A forty-year-old woman climbed into my passenger seat, and we introduced ourselves to each other. We had a great time of sharing in the car on the twenty-minute drive to her home, and she mentioned being a single mother of three children. She was happy to hear my thankful testimony and also shared her testimony of surviving health issues and overcoming adversity with God's help. As she was facing challenges with her own children at the time, she connected with my story of dealing with a difficult teen. We had a mutually encouraging conversation and spoke like old friends. In fact she didn't want to get out of the car right away, when we finally arrived at her house. Before getting out of the car, she probably spoke with me for an additional fifteen minutes, and I prayed with her before she departed.

"Thank you, Lord," I whispered with joy in my heart on my drive home.

I knew that God must have had something better in mind when the car didn't start, even though I had fervently believed that my prayer for the car to start would be answered. On my drive home, I called the security team at the college and checked on the status of the woman who waited with her vehicle, since I wanted to make sure that she was able to get safely home. As it turned out, she had insisted that the two guys on the security team should try again with the automatic car starter. When one of the security guards went out to help, he happened to notice a loose bolt and tightened it. The car started immediately after that, and the woman was able to drive herself home. I was tickled to learn that God had answered my prayer after all, but only after I had taken the other lady home. God must have wanted her to hear about the Thankful Principle.

Another night, I had planned to go straight home after work, but an unplanned stop in the faculty workroom led to an encounter with a co-worker. I ended up mentioning the Thankful Principle to her, and she responded, "I really needed to hear that tonight." It turned out that she was stressed out with juggling two jobs, college coursework, young children, and a potential medical issue. She told me that she planned to try the Thankful Principle, and I told her that I expected to hear a great report the next time I saw her. When I did see her a few days later, I asked, "So what's the good report?" She then told me that she had been given a great medical report that a suspicious lump was not cancerous. We rejoiced together.

Over the next few weeks, it seemed that God was giving me opportunities to share and to also hear great reports. It had begun happening so often, I was more desirous than ever to keep sharing. If I felt the prompting of the Lord, I would say something, even if I only had time to say an encouraging word about the need to be thankful, according to Philippians 4.

At a women's brunch at church one morning, I was speaking with a friend about writing my book on thankfulness. Another lady, whom I had never met before, sat across from us and was interested in learning more. I told her a bit about my initial testimony of dealing with my teenage daughter, and she told me that she believed God had placed me at her table. It turned out that she had been discouraged and was going through similar issues with her troubled teenage daughter. My story was just what she needed to hear for a word of encouragement. Without initially knowing why, I had even shared details of my story that I didn't normally share with others, but after learning about her situation, I knew that God had prompted me to share those specific details for a reason.

A student and I talked about the Thankful Principle one night, and I learned that her family had been dealing with her husband's lack of steady employment for two years, although he had found temporary work here and there. Normally, this student attended a daytime class of mine, but I knew God must have sent her to my night class that evening to talk to me. She was excited to learn about the Thankful Principle and went home and told her husband about it. The following week, she told me that she had faced a challenging situation at work that would have normally made her angry, but she began thanking God for the situation. As it turned out, the situation resolved to a favorable outcome for her, and she was excited about the results.

After the wedding, Danielle had also begun telling me about situations where she was applying the Thankful Principle in her marriage. One morning, she was in an angry mood and frustrated over the amount of time her husband was spending on playing video games. In frustration, she began thanking God for the situation and thanked God that he could show Eric that it was a problem without her having to resort to nagging him about it. About the same time that she had finished praying quietly in the other room, Eric walked in. He had suddenly stopped playing the game without her saying a word to him, and she was happy to discover that taking matters to God was much nicer than arguing and nagging. Another time on a lengthy car ride with her family, she recognized that she needed to begin quietly thanking God. When she did, she was able to diffuse a situation that might have normally escalated into an argument. Thanking God brought her peace and prevented her from overreacting. I was proud of her spiritual growth and enjoyed hearing about how she was using this spiritual weapon.

Danielle wasn't the only family member putting the Thankful Principle into practice. One morning when we were together, my son casually mentioned to me that he had started to have a negative attitude at work one night. Jacob was working a couple of part-time jobs at the time, including working as a banquet server at a fancy hotel. He had learned at the last minute that he would have to serve at the head table for a bridal party. He was unhappy about having to hastily grab the certain needed items in less time than he would have normally had to set things up. When he realized that he was allowing himself to grow angry, he decided to try thanking God for the situation. Not only did he lose the negativity, but he received his largest tip ever that night, which almost doubled his pay for the evening.

My South African friend, Ellen, and I talked online, and I asked if she was still using the Thankful Principle. She shared that the school that she worked for had no funds, and it looked like the department of education was not keen on sponsoring the project she was working on anymore. She added the following details:

"I hadn't been paid in two months, but I remained thankful each day and believed God would come through for me in the midst of everything. I was calm at times and got anxious in some moments, but being thankful made me to see God as the Father he is in my life. I am back at work and got paid my two months of salary owed to me and am continuing to be thankful."

I was happy to hear Ellen's good report and to know that she was still applying the Thankful Principle in her life. It seemed everywhere I went, I kept bumping into people who needed the good news of the Thankful Principle. Even online and over the phone, God had me sharing my testimony with several other people and telling them about it. Some thanked me for the reminder, and others were inspired enough to tell me that they would try it.

CHAPTER TWENTY-FIVE
BEST INTERESTS AT HEART

AFTER MONTHS OF GOING WITHOUT a job interview, I snagged one in late September for a junior high mathematics position at a small rural school. After interviewing, I was about 50/50 on whether I even wanted the job because the commute would have been a 45-minute drive each way. Six days later, I was called and told that I had not been selected for the position. Part of me was relieved about not having the long commute, but my ego was bruised because I was not picked. Although I was trying to remain thankful, something within me continued feeling rejected and hurt. Why wasn't I good enough? Why was someone else a better candidate? I wrestled with such thoughts in between trying to be optimistic and thankful. I continued to thank God that I didn't get that job because it wasn't the right one for me, but it was hard to remain upbeat.

The next day, as I was feeling a bit philosophical on the matter, I posted the following status on my Facebook account: "There are times in our lives when we face disappointments with a sense of hurt, rejection, or depression; however, when we can embrace the fact that God has our best interests at heart, we can find joy in the journey." I also added the following scripture: "*Trust in the LORD with all your heart and lean not on your own understanding; in all your ways acknowledge him, and he will make your paths straight,*" (Proverbs 3:5-6, NIV).

The thought that "God has my best interests at heart" really played over and over again in my mind, as I meditated on the significance of the words I had shared with my friends. All day long and throughout the next few days, I kept thinking to myself, "God has my best interests at heart. God has my best interests at heart." I began to say it out loud, and then I began to firmly believe it. Yes, I knew it to be true all along; however, a stark difference exists between knowing something to be true in theory and actually believing it in the heart. A weight was lifted, and I could embrace that fact and be joyful even when something didn't work out the way I had planned. God knew best, and I would trust him.

Over the next couple of weeks, I had two more teaching job interviews. Each job interview was seemingly leading to a better paying position than the previous interview. In the second and third interviews, I shared the Thankful Principle with the people who interviewed me for public school positions. At the third interview, the principal and two assistant principals (all Christians) took notes on the scripture passage I shared and one vice-principal even joked that I would thank God for my students' crummy attitudes. When I walked out of that interview, I was joyful and told God that I didn't even care if I got the job or not. If I had accomplished nothing else, I felt happy that I was able to share the Thankful Principle with them, and that was enough.

It seemed strange that after only one job interview over the summer, I suddenly had three interviews within an 18-day period. Was God opening a door for me or trying to teach me something more about trusting him? I began to thank God that he was in control over the situation, my finances, and my career, and I could rest easy in knowing that God had my best interests at heart.

When none of the interviews led to a job, I still remained at peace. While I prayed and continued to trust God, I began to realize that he wanted me to concentrate on writing. If I had the responsibility of a full-time job, I wouldn't have the luxury of available time needed to devote to the additional projects I was already planning to write. By continuing to teach and tutor part-time at the college, I could fulfill my desire to teach, but I would still have time to work on various writing projects.

Although my life-changing journey into thankfulness is still a work in progress, I am learning daily how to make a thankful attitude my first response, rather than an afterthought. It didn't happen overnight, but embracing the Thankful Principle has been powerful and effective in dealing with difficult circumstances. It allows God to work in any situation to change me, the situation, or both. Time and again, God has been faithful when I pray with a thankful heart and bring each concern to him.

Anxiety cannot remain when we make our requests known to God with thanksgiving. Peace will always follow. Don't just take my word for it. If you have committed your life to Jesus Christ, God will do the same for you.

"*Be joyful always; pray continually; give thanks*

in all circumstances; for this is God's will for you in Christ Jesus" (I Thessalonians 5:16-18, NIV).

ABOUT THE AUTHOR

   Marcia Day Brown is a happily married mother of four grown children. Her early years were spent in a variety of places, since her father, Dr. Gene G. Day, was an Air Force chaplain. When she was ten, her family moved to Parsons, Kansas, where her parents continued in ministry. She graduated in 1985 from Evangel University with a B.S. degree in Elementary Education. In addition to working in a variety of teaching jobs, she enjoyed 17 years of successful freelance writing for Argus Communications (poster, greeting card, and calendar editorial and concept writing), 6 years as a newspaper columnist for the *Evansville Courier,* and is currently involved in editing and consulting projects. She currently lives in Indianapolis, Indiana, and teaches developmental mathematics at a community college. She enjoys traveling, spending time with her family, and playing the piano.

Made in the USA
Columbia, SC
17 January 2024